THE OFFICIAL GUIDE

Published in 2023 by Welbeck
An imprint of Welbeck Non-Fiction Limited, part of Welbeck Publishing Group.
20 Mortimer Street
London W1T 3JW
www.welbeckpublishing.com

A CIP catalogue record for this book is available from the British Library

ISBN: 978-1-80279-636-0

Editor: Conor Kilgallon
Design: Luke Griffin, Russell Knowles
Picture Research: Paul Langan
Production: Rachel Burgess

Printed in Dubai

10 9 8 7 6 5 4 3 2 1

All facts and statistics in this book are correct as at 1st March 2023.

THE OFFICIAL GUIDE

SIMON COLLINGS

Above: Teams will once again compete for the Webb Ellis Cup at Rugby World Cup 2023.

Contents

Introduction

Since the very first Rugby World Cup back in 1987, the game has continued to grow and fans have been entertained by the biggest stars coming together to compete on the grandest stage of all. Rugby World Cup 2023 promises to be no different, with France hosting the tournament once again, having done so in 2007.

Rugby World Cup 2023 is the 10th edition of the tournament and it has set its sights on being bigger and better than ever before.

Tournament organisers have made a record 2.6 million tickets available as part of their plans to make it the most accessible Rugby World Cup ever.

France hosted a Rugby World Cup before back in 2007, but this tournament promises to be on another scale to that, as the organisers look to raise the bar of fan experience, sustainability and player welfare.

"There are steps forward with every tournament, but Rugby World Cup 2023 is certainly taking a giant leap for rugby," said World Rugby Chairman Sir Bill Beaumont, speaking one year out from the tournament starting.

"I have no doubt that it will be a transformative and spectacular event for fans with superb stadia, hugely engaged host cities and a celebratory feel as we mark 200 years of rugby."

A total of nine stadia will host matches at Rugby World Cup 2023 and, as they are spread out across France, they will provide fans with the chance to take in all of the country.

Above: France proved to be brilliant hosts of Rugby World Cup 2007.

The stadia are a mixture of modern and classic venues and promise to add to the spectacle of the tournament.

Rugby fans will no doubt take the time while in France to soak up all the country's culture – particularly its fine food – and it certainly proved a popular destination for supporters back in 2007.

The game itself, however, has moved on since then and this tournament should be one of the most competitive ever.

There is little to choose from between the top sides in the world, while the fact that Chile have qualified for their first-ever Rugby World Cup underlines how the game is growing all over the world.

That is a key aim of World Rugby, and the emergence of a side like Chile shows just how much the game has evolved since the very first Rugby World Cup back in 1987.

Chile and their fans will be hoping 2023 is a year they never forget, but the same goes for many sides competing in France.

That is certainly the case for the hosts, who will be dreaming of winning their first-ever Rugby World Cup and hoping that the support of a home crowd could make all the difference.

If history has shown us anything, though, it is that it is often hard to pick a winner – and this tournament should be no different.

A year out from Rugby World Cup 2019, few backed South Africa to go all the way, but they were the team that lifted the Webb Ellis Cup in Japan.

The Springboks want to retain their crown in France, but the competition is fierce, as the likes of Australia, England, Ireland and New Zealand have their eyes on the prize, too.

Whoever ends up winning, it promises to be a captivating tournament and *Rugby World Cup France 2023: The Official Guide* has all the information a fan could need.

Above: Makazole Mapimpi is congratulated by his teammates after scoring a try as South Africa beat England to win Rugby World Cup 2019.

RUGBY
2007
SOCIE

WELCOME TO FRANCE

Ever since the first Rugby World Cup back in 1987, the game has continued to grow every year. France were hosts back in 2007 and put on a brilliant show then, during a tournament that was full of drama and shocks. Rugby World Cup 2023 promises to be no different and visiting fans will be treated to stunning stadia across France. The country is excited to showcase what it has to offer and everyone is welcome for what should be a memorable ride.

Left: France stunned New Zealand with a fine performance in the quarter-finals of Rugby World Cup 2007.

About Rugby World Cup 2023

The organisers of Rugby World Cup 2023 have set ambitious targets both on and off the pitch to ensure this tournament is the biggest yet. Crucial to their plans is a desire to leave a lasting legacy long after the tournament ends. Rugby World Cup 2023 is about far more than 48 matches, as it bids to make a real difference.

With every tournament, Rugby World Cup has grown in size, and France 2023 promises to be no different.

Tournament organisers have set themselves bold targets, making 2.6 million tickets available as part of their attempts to beat previous attendance records.

The demand for tickets has been unprecedented, and it is anticipated around 600,000 fans will travel to France for the tournament, staying for on average 15 days in the country.

The support within France itself has been huge as well, though, and that much was made clear by a study published by World Rugby one year out from the tournament's start date. It revealed how a host nation has never been so engaged with the tournament and that nine out of 10 French people support the country hosting Rugby World Cup 2023.

The aim for the game is to build on the great success of Rugby World Cup 2019 in Japan. That tournament attracted two million new participants to the sport; achieved a 99 per cent attendance rate; set a new fan zone attendance record of 1.13 million; and delivered a record nationwide economic impact of £4.3 billion.

France plans to make a similar impression and key to their plans is ensuring that Rugby World Cup 2023 has a lasting legacy, which stretches way beyond the 48 matches taking place.

"The adventure of this Rugby World Cup 2023 shall endure afterwards, in our clubs, our territories, in our society for generations to come," said France 2023 Chairman Jacques Rivoal.

Above: Rugby World Cup 2007 proved to be a huge hit with fans, who loved visiting France.

Above: France boasts plenty of stunning stadia, such as the Stade Vélodrome in Marseille.

"Until the last whistle blows, our priority will be to think about everything to come post-2023 and to make the event's positive impact a tangible reality."

Rivoal's words underline the growth of rugby since the first tournament in 1987 and how a Rugby World Cup is now about much more than what happens on the pitch.

The organisers of Rugby World Cup 2023 have made four commitments to their legacy: acting for a sustainable and circular economy; investing in education, training and employment; reducing our impact on the environment; and fostering inclusion and accessibility.

The economic impact of the tournament should be great, with an anticipated €2 billion (£1.7 billion) due to be directly generated in the whole country, with the profits of that entirely devoted to financing projects to develop rugby. Some 17,000 jobs are also due to be created in France by hosting Rugby World Cup 2023.

A key element of the economic impact, however, is sustainability. As a result, every stadium at the tournament will seek to promote local and healthy food, which will celebrate French gastronomy.

Tournament organisers have created the Gastronomic Squad – a team of 23 French chefs, who will be challenged with designing menus which will be offered during the tournament that feature natural, unprocessed foods and a short supply chain.

Sustainability runs throughout France's Rugby World Cup plans – and that even applies to the medals the players will receive. Phones and other electronic products will be collected in the build-up to the tournament. They will then be sorted and the precious metals extracted and melted down to create the medals for the winners, runners-up and third place team at Rugby World Cup 2023.

Rugby World Cups often inspire the next generation and France plan to help the stars of tomorrow on their way with the creation of Campus 2023. It is an apprentice training centre, which involves 1,200 tutors helping young men and women between the ages of 18 and 30. They will be trained for careers in sport, tourism and security management, with the idea being that the jobs and skills they obtain last way beyond the tournament.

Youth is a key part of France's plans to deliver a record-breaking tournament and nowhere will that be more evident than with the singing of the national anthems.

Before kick-off, a choir made up of children from the project La Mêlée des Chœurs will sing the national anthems of the teams. There will be 26 choirs of 300 children each, with more than 7,000 youngsters participating.

The anthems will also be performed in sign language as part of the tournament organisers' desire to champion inclusivity and emphasise how rugby really is a game for everyone.

Setting the scene for Rugby World Cup 2023

The Trophy Tour of France gave fans all over the country the chance to see the Webb Ellis Cup and experience the magic of a Rugby World Cup. Excitement has been building in France ever since they were named hosts of the tournament and once again volunteers will get to play a key role in ensuring the competition is a great success.

When they visit France, rugby fans will quickly learn that travelling by train is a great way to see all of the country. France boasts an excellent rail network and fittingly that was the way that the Webb Ellis Cup was paraded around the country as part of the Trophy Tour.

Like Rugby World Cup 2023 itself, the Trophy Tour was very ambitious, as it comprised visits to 51 towns and cities in France across 114 days.

The Tour began its journey in Lille in July 2022 before ending up in Paris in November, which is where the final of Rugby World Cup 2023 will be held.

Visitors at Lille train station in July 2022 will have spotted the Rugby World Cup 2023 exhibition train, which gave supporters a taste of what to expect at the tournament and looked back on previous editions, too. Famous jerseys and memorabilia from past Rugby World Cups adorned the walls of carriages on the train, while an immersive virtual reality experience allowed fans to feel what the Stade de France will be like for the opening match in 2023.

The Webb Ellis Cup was, of course, the star attraction and after leaving Lille it travelled all over France so fans could see it.

The Tour underlined the excitement in France at the country being hosts and, as has been the case at past tournaments, volunteers will play a vital role. They will be involved in every part of Rugby World Cup 2023 from public welcome, tournament services, accreditations, communication and marketing activities, media operations and the tournament's sports presentation.

In keeping with how rugby is a game for everyone, Rugby World Cup 2023's volunteer programme was opened to both French and international applicants, of all ages and backgrounds, including people with disabilities.

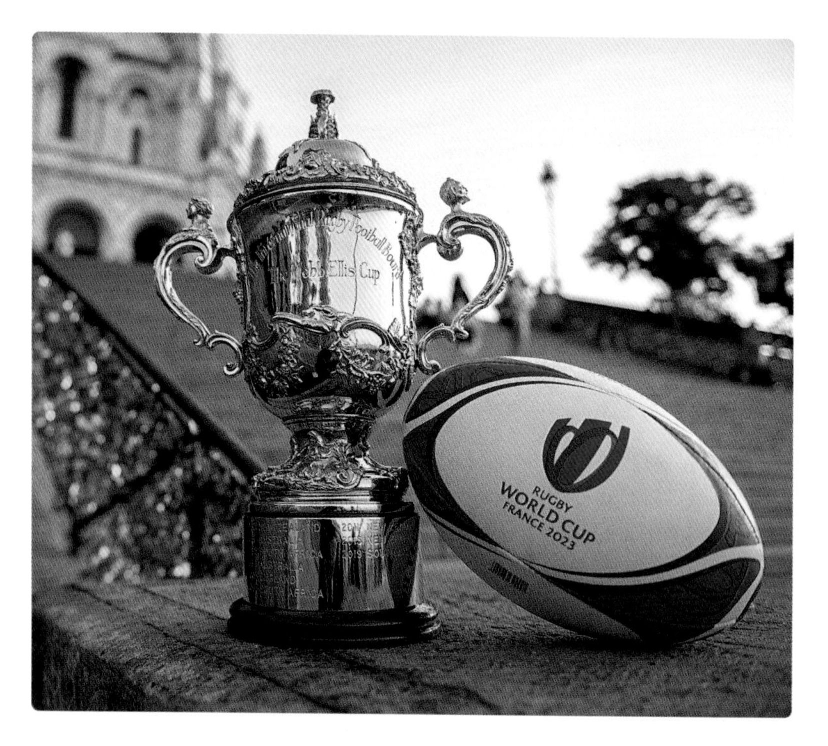

Left: The Webb Ellis Cup and match ball in Paris to mark one year until Rugby World Cup 2023.

Know the tournament

Pool phase

The tournament's 20 nations have been drawn into four pools of five teams. Each team will play the other teams in its pool on a round-robin basis. The following number of points will be awarded for each match:

Win: 4 points
Draw: 2 points
Loss: 0 points
4 or more tries: 1 point
Loss by 7 points or fewer: 1 point

At the completion of the pool phase, the teams in a pool are ranked one to five based on their cumulative match points and identified respectively as winners, runner-up, third, fourth and fifth. The winner and runner-up in each pool qualify for the quarter-finals. The top three teams of each pool will also earn automatic qualification to Rugby World Cup 2027.

If at the completion of the pool phase two or more teams are level on match points, then the following criteria shall be used in the following order until one of the teams can be determined as the higher ranked:

- The winner of the match between the two tied teams shall be ranked higher.
- The team which has the best difference between points for and points against during all its pool matches shall be ranked higher.
- The team which has the best difference between tries scored for and tries scored against during all its pool matches shall be ranked higher.
- The team which has scored the most points in all its pool matches shall be ranked higher.
- The team which has scored the most tries in all its pool matches shall be ranked higher.
- Should the tie be unresolved at the conclusion of all above steps then the rankings, as per the updated official World Rugby Men's Rankings powered by Capgemini on 9 October, 2023, shall determine the higher-ranked team.

Knockout matches

If teams are tied at full-time, the winner shall be determined through the following sequential criteria:

- Extra time: Following an interval of five minutes, extra time of 10 minutes each way (with an interval of five minutes) shall be played in full.
- Sudden death: If the scores are tied at the conclusion of extra time, and following an interval of five minutes, then a further extra time of 10 minutes maximum shall be played. During this period the first team to score any points shall be declared the winner.
- Kicking competition: If after the sudden death period no winner can be declared, a kicking competition will be organised between the two teams. The winner of that competition shall be declared the winner of the match.

Quarter-finals

The top two teams from each pool will progress to the last eight and the quarter-final line-ups will be determined in the following way:

QF1: Winner of Pool C v Runner-up Pool D
QF2: Winner of Pool B v Runner-up Pool A
QF3: Winner of Pool D v Runner-up Pool C
QF4: Winner of Pool A v Runner-up Pool B

Semi-finals

The semi-final line-ups will be decided in the following manner:

SF1: Winner QF1 v Winner QF2
SF2: Winner QF3 v Winner QF4

Bronze final

This match will be contested between the two losing semi-finalists.

The final

This match will be contested between the two winning semi-finalists.

Below: New Zealand performing the haka is always a great spectacle at a Rugby World Cup.

The rugby heritage of France

Rugby was first played in France over 150 years ago and the game has grown massively since then. The sport is now hugely popular in the country, particularly in the south west, and Rugby World Cup 2023 will be the second time France has hosted the tournament. Winning the Webb Ellis Cup would be the perfect addition to France's rich history.

The story goes that it was all the way back in 1823 that the game of rugby was born. A young William Webb Ellis was playing a game of football at Rugby School, when legend has it he picked the ball up and started running.

From that moment, rugby was born, but it was not until some 50 years later that it began to emerge in France. Unsurprisingly, it was the influence of English people living in the country that led to the sport's growth in the port town of Le Havre. They formed a club there in 1872 – Le Havre Athletic Club – and while today it is regarded as a football team, its origins were very different.

Above: Serge Blanco scores a famous try against Australia at Rugby World Cup 1987.

Back in 1872 it is reported that the participants played a hybrid of rugby and football, 'combination' as it has been dubbed, while people also took part in athletics.

This development sowed the first seeds for rugby in France and it was not long before two of the rugby powerhouses of today, Racing 92 and Stade Français, were formed; in 1892 they competed in what many consider to have been the first-ever French rugby championship.

Racing took the title and the popularity of the game was growing in France, so much so that the sport was played in the Paris Olympics of 1900. France were pioneers for the game at that time, playing alongside Germany and Great Britain, and they claimed the gold medal.

By 1910, competition in rugby was increasing and France joined the Five Nations tournament to play alongside England, Ireland, Scotland and Wales. It was a big moment for the country and, by the end of the decade, further roots were laid down thanks to the formation of the Fédération Française de Rugby, the game's governing body in France.

After being ousted from the Five Nations in 1931 because of allegations of professionalism in a sport that was still amateur, France returned to the

Above: France's "champagne rugby" has led them to three finals, including this one in 2011 against the All Blacks.

competition in 1947 after World War II and it was during the 1950s that they enjoyed success. They tied for the championship in 1954 and 1955, before claiming their first outright triumph in 1959.

It was around this time that France were becoming known for their flamboyant style of rugby and some say it was then that the famous phrase 'champagne rugby' was first coined. Either way, it has become synonymous with France, and other attacking teams, as summed up by fly-half Thierry Lacroix's words at Rugby World Cup 1995.

He had just kicked 26 points to fire France to victory over Ireland, but he was less than satisfied.

"We are capable of playing champagne rugby, but we are still trying to get the cork out," Lacroix said.

France have dazzled at times during their history and they have been successful too, taking their tally of Six Nations titles to 10 in 2022 by winning the Grand Slam. They have been responsible for some of the most famous Rugby World Cup moments as well, from Serge Blanco's stunning try against Australia in 1987 to their thrilling comeback versus New Zealand in 1999.

France have always sought to entertain and that certainly goes for their their clubs in the Top 14, which is one of the most exciting and competitive leagues in the world.

The core of teams for that league come from the south of France, and that is where the game is most strongly supported. There is a special connection between the south of France and rugby, which is difficult to put your finger on, but the love can be summed up in a little village called Larrivière-Saint-Savin.

There, you will find a chapel which is dedicated specifically to rugby and has been dubbed Notre Dame de Rugby, with fans able to visit and write messages in a visitors' book.

"This church is a place of worship for rugby fans the world over," Morgan Bignet, curator at the chapel, told Reuters in 2015.

The challenge for France's current generation is to write the next, exciting chapter in the history of French rugby. Under the current coaching setup, France have trusted in youth, and their style of rugby is one of pace and power.

There is still more than an element of flair to their game too, which is a throwback to famous teams of the past.

Now the aim is for this France team to ensure the champagne is flowing both on and off the pitch at Rugby World Cup 2023.

Match venues

In total, nine stadia will play host to the 48 matches being played at Rugby World Cup 2023. They are located all across France and will allow supporters the opportunity to explore different parts of the country when they visit. The tournament boasts some of the most modern stadia in the world and also others that are steeped in history.

STADIUMS

1. .... Stade de Bordeaux
2. .... Stade Pierre-Mauroy
3. .... OL Stadium
4. .... Stade Vélodrome
5. .... Stade de la Beaujoire
6. .... Stade de Nice
7. .... Stade de France
8. .... Stade Geoffroy-Guichard
9. .... Stadium de Toulouse

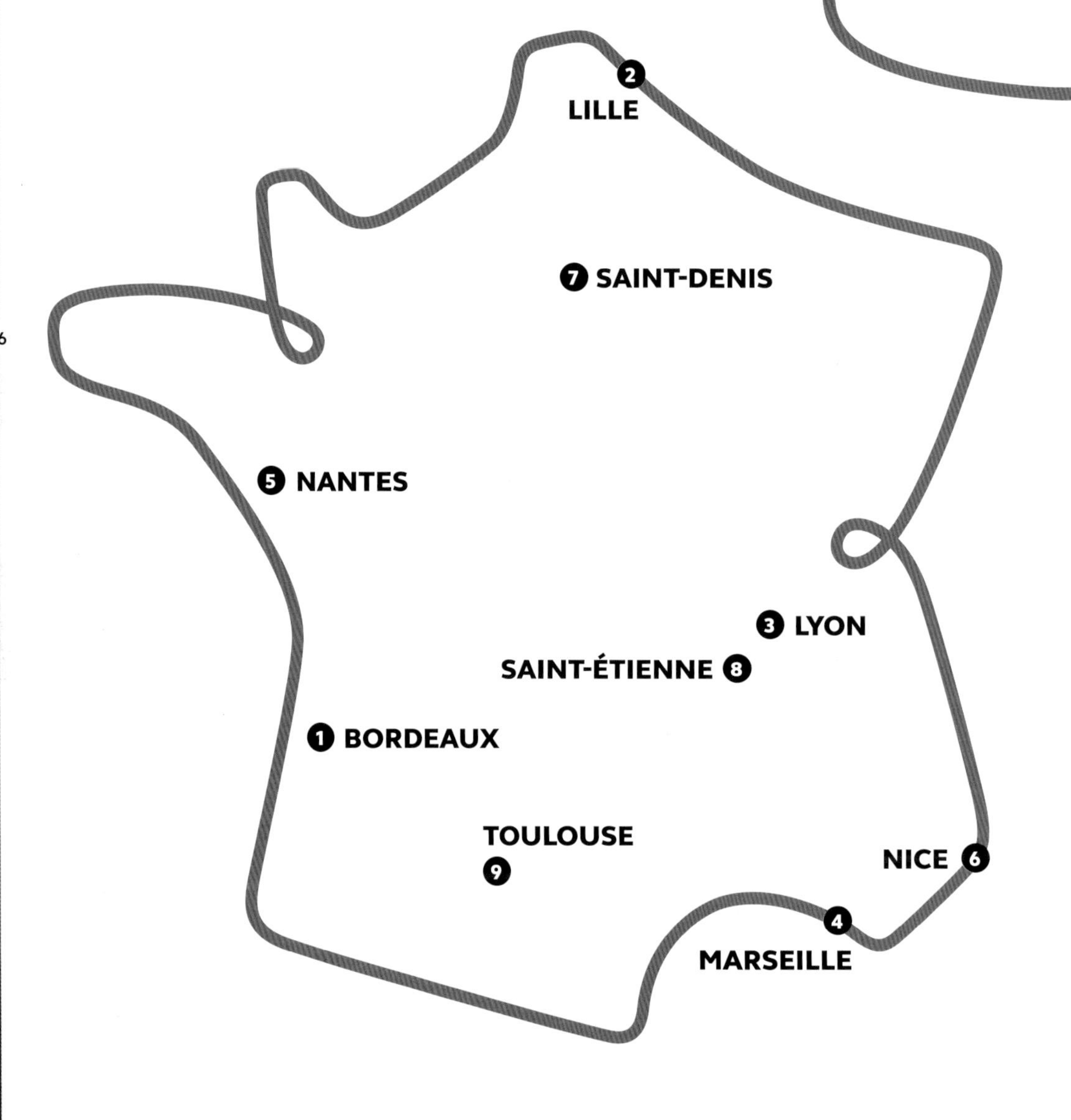

Stade de Bordeaux

Usually the home of French football side Girondins de Bordeaux, the venue is still no stranger to hosting rugby as well. The stadium opened in May 2015 and just weeks later it staged the semi-finals of the Top 14, as ASM Clermont Auvergne beat Stade Toulousain to reach the final. It also hosted the semi-finals again in 2019, this time for the clash between Stade Toulousain and Stade Rochelais, and the crowd of 42,071 remains the stadium's record attendance.

The venue is an ultra-modern arena and its design is incredibly striking, with long plinths all around the structure. The architects decided to incorporate these in their design as a nod to the slender pine trees of the region's Landes forest.

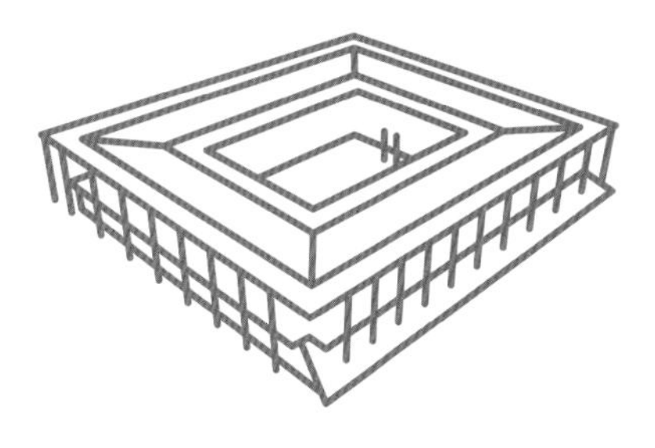

Location: .... Bordeaux
Capacity: 42,060

The Stade de Bordeaux is used to being part of major tournaments, as it was one of the grounds selected for the Euro 2016 football tournament, proving to be a big hit with visiting fans. It staged five matches then and will host the same number at Rugby World Cup 2023.

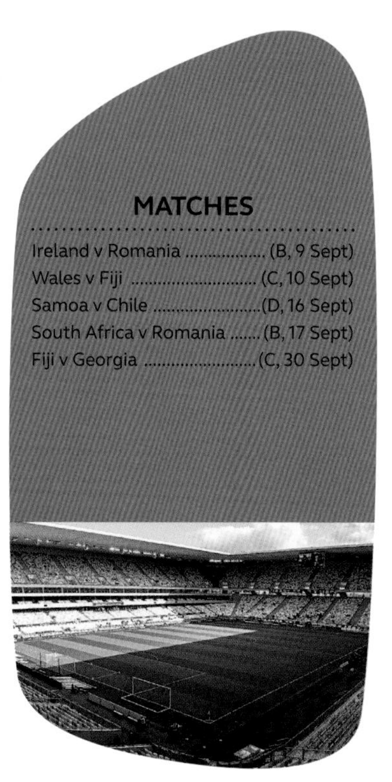

MATCHES

Ireland v Romania .... (B, 9 Sept)
Wales v Fiji .... (C, 10 Sept)
Samoa v Chile ....(D, 16 Sept)
South Africa v Romania .... (B, 17 Sept)
Fiji v Georgia .... (C, 30 Sept)

Stade Pierre-Mauroy

There is not a more innovative stadium at Rugby World Cup 2023 than the Stade Pierre-Mauroy. From the outside it appears to be a typical stadium, but it is much more.

The venue is normally used to host football, as French side LOSC (Lille Olympique Sporting Club) play their home matches there, but it has staged rugby, too. It can, however, host all manner of events, thanks to the ingenious design of its pitch inside the arena. One half of the pitch lifts up on hydraulics and then slides over the other, leaving a hard-surfaced bowl behind. That can then be used for a range of things and the Stade Pierre-Mauroy has as a result staged basketball, tennis and music, too.

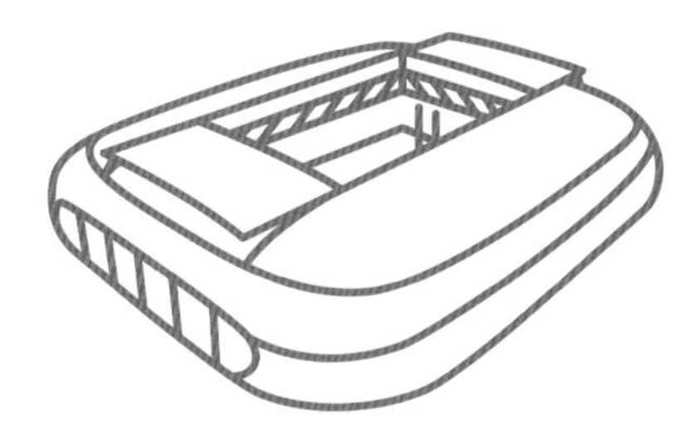

Location: .... Lille
Capacity: 50,096

Situated in Lille, the area has a rich rugby history, as back at Rugby World Cup 1991 it was a host city. The nearby Stade du Nord hosted New Zealand's quarter-final win over Canada, with the Stade Pierre-Mauroy not opened until 2012.

MATCHES

France v Uruguay ....(A, 14 Sept)
England v Chile .... (D, 23 Sept)
Scotland v Romania ....(B, 30 Sept)
England v Samoa .... (D, 7 Oct)
Tonga v Romania ....(B, 8 Oct)

OL Stadium

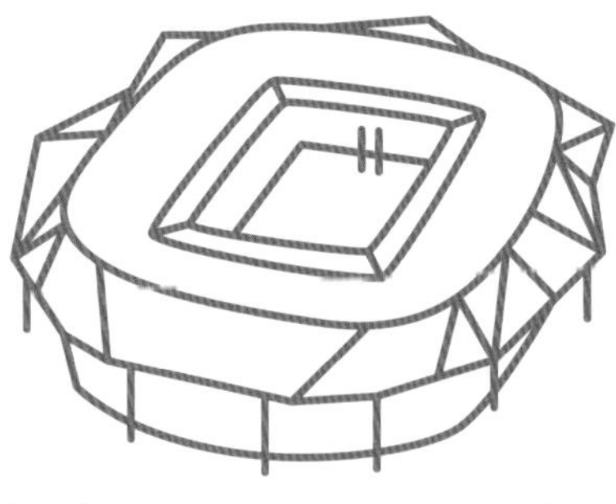

Location: .... Lyon
Capacity: 58,883

The third biggest stadium at Rugby World Cup 2023, and one of the most modern, the OL Stadium is unsurprisingly hosting some big games at the tournament. Wales v Australia will kick off the action there in a region that has a strong rugby history.

The Stade de Gerland hosted matches at Rugby World Cup 2007 and Lyon has once again been picked as a host, although this time the OL Stadium will be used. It was opened in January 2016 and has since been used for several major events. The European Champions Cup and Challenge Cup finals have been played there, while a France XV played New Zealand there in 2017.

The ground, which is the home of French football side Olympique Lyonnais, was used as a venue at Euro 2016 and three years later when France hosted the FIFA Women's World Cup. It boasts one of the most modern pitches around as it uses hybrid turf, which involves natural grass being woven into synthetic fibres to create a more durable surface.

MATCHES

Wales v Australia ....(C, 24 Sept)
Uruguay v Namibia ....(A, 27 Sept)
New Zealand v Italy ....(A, 29 Sept)
New Zealand v Uruguay ....(A, 5 Oct)
France v Italy ....(A, 6 Oct)

Stade Vélodrome

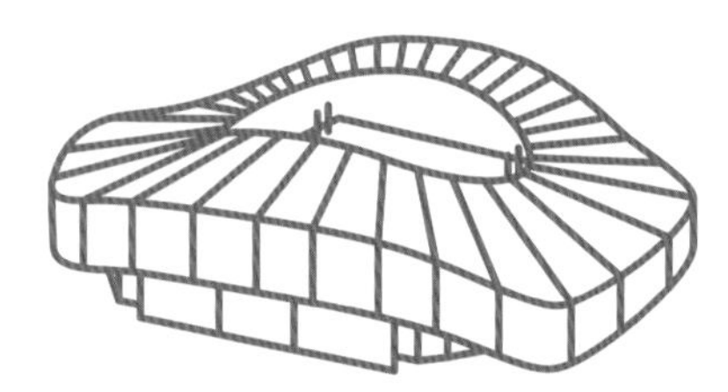

Location: .... Marseille
Capacity: 67,847

Stade Vélodrome is one of the most iconic and historic stadia in France and has been hosting major events for nearly 100 years. First opened in 1937, it was used for the FIFA World Cup just a year later. The venue has since undergone renovations and improvements, most notably before the football World Cup in 1998 and Euro 2016, and it now boasts a capacity of 67,847. That makes it the largest French club football stadium in the country, and it will be the second-biggest venue at Rugby World Cup 2023.

Usually the home of French football side Olympique de Marseille, the venue does have strong ties to rugby. It first staged a test match in 2000, when France beat New Zealand, and Les Bleus have since returned repeatedly to what has been a happy hunting ground for them.

Stade Vélodrome hosted two quarter-finals during Rugby World Cup 2007 and it will do the same this time around.

MATCHES

England v Argentina ....(D, 9 Sept)
South Africa v Scotland ......(B, 10 Sept)
France v Namibia ....(A, 21 Sept)
South Africa v Tonga ....(B, 1 Oct)
Quarter-final 1 ....(14 Oct)
Quarter-final 3 ....(15 Oct)

Stade de la Beaujoire

Stade de la Beaujoire may be best known for being the home of French football side FC Nantes, but it has a rich rugby history, too. The venue was chosen to be part of Rugby World Cup 2007 and it played host to one of the tournament's most iconic matches, as Fiji pipped Wales 38-34 in a brilliant game.

Back in 2007, Stade de la Beaujoire hosted three matches and this time it will stage one more, with organisers hoping for plenty of fireworks during the games there. The venue has regularly been used for marquee competitions and it was part of the Euro 1984 football tournament in the same year that it officially opened. It was also used for the FIFA World Cup in 1998.

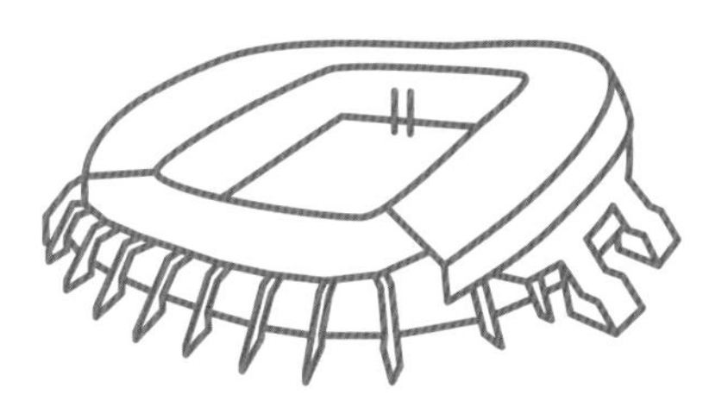

Location: .... Nantes
Capacity: 35,520

In its early years, when supporters could stand on the terraces during games, this venue used to hold around 50,000 spectators, but it was renovated in 1998 before the FIFA World Cup to become an all-seater arena with a capacity of around 35,000.

MATCHES

Ireland v Tonga .... (B, 16 Sept)
Argentina v Chile .... (D, 30 Sept)
Wales v Georgia .... (C, 7 Oct)
Japan v Argentina .... (D 8 Oct)

Stade de Nice

Located just outside the city of Nice, this venue is one of the most stunning on show at Rugby World Cup 2023. Opened in 2013, its modern design is eye-catching and the backdrop of the French countryside only adds to its spectacle.

The home ground of French football side OGC Nice, it was used as part of the Euro 2016 football tournament and also played a key role in the hosting of the FIFA Women's World Cup three years later. The venue has been used for rugby in the past too, with France playing Scotland there in 2019 and club side Stade Toulousain also opting to play some games there.

However, Rugby World Cup 2023 will be the first time this stadium has hosted major rugby matches for a competition of this stature. In total Stade de Nice will host four matches, including England's encounter with Japan.

The venue is also home to the National Sport Museum of France, which supporters can visit as part of their trip.

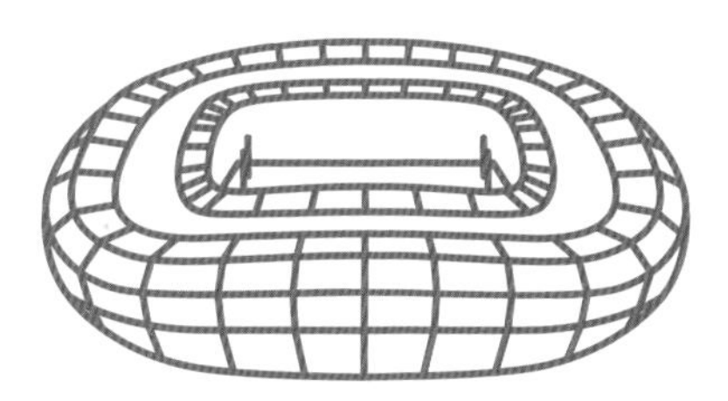

Location: .... Nice
Capacity: 35,983

MATCHES

Wales v Portugal .... (C, 16 Sept)
England v Japan .... (D, 17 Sept
Italy v Uruguay .... (A, 20 Sept)
Scotland v Tonga .... (B, 24 Sept)

Stade de France

Built ahead of the FIFA World Cup in 1998, the Stade de France is one of the most iconic sporting venues in Europe. It is also one of the biggest too, with the ground holding more than 80,000 supporters. Used by the French national team for both football and rugby, it is regarded as one of the most atmospheric and noisiest stadia around.

Since hosting the FIFA World Cup final in 1998, which France won by beating Brazil 3-0, the Stade de France has been used for many major events, including the final of Euro 2016 and Champions League finals.

The venue played a key role the last time France hosted a Rugby World Cup back in 2007, and it will do so again this time. It will be hosting 10 matches during the tournament, including both semi-finals, the bronze final and the final. It will also kick-off the competition with the highly anticipated encounter between France and New Zealand.

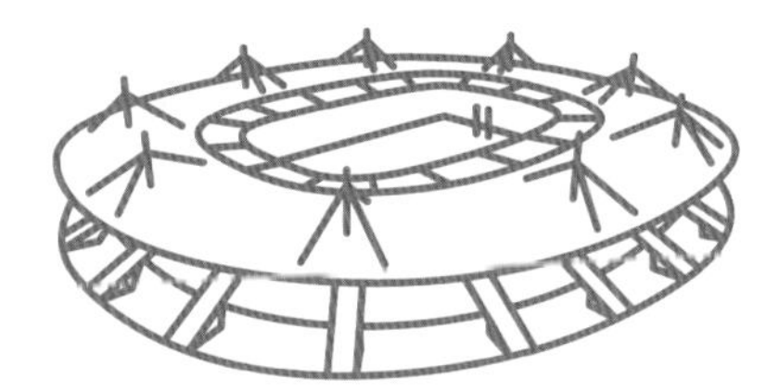

Location: .... Saint-Denis (Paris)
Capacity: 80,023

MATCHES

France v New Zealand .... (A, 8 Sept)
Australia v Georgia .... (C, 9 Sept)
South Africa v Ireland .... (B, 23 Sept)
Ireland v Scotland .... (B, 7 Oct)
Quarter-final 2 .... (14 Oct)
Quarter-final 4 .... (15 Oct)
Semi-final 1 .... (20 Oct)
Semi-final 2 .... (21 Oct)
Bronze final .... (27 Oct)
Final .... (28 Oct)

Above: The Stade de France previously hosted the Rugby World Cup final between England and South Africa in 2007.

Stade Geoffroy-Guichard

Stade Geoffroy-Guichard may be the oldest stadium at Rugby World Cup 2023, but it also boasts one of the best atmospheres. It is the home of French football side AS Saint-Étienne and has the nickname "Le Chaudron" (The Cauldron) due to the noise that fans create on match day.

The design of the stadium certainly helps to create a brilliant atmosphere. Originally the venue had a running track, but that was removed in 1956 and thus fans were allowed to be closer to the pitch. All four stands at the ground are now also linked, with no gaps, meaning noise stays inside the venue instead of escaping out.

Originally built and used for football, the Stade Geoffroy-Guichard is now used to hosting rugby and France played their first game there back in 2001 when they beat Fiji 77-10. At Rugby World Cup 2007 it hosted three pool matches and has gained an extra one for this tournament.

Location: .... Saint-Étienne
Capacity: 42,152

MATCHES

Italy v Namibia (A, 9 Sept)
Australia v Fiji (C, 17 Sept)
Argentina v Samoa (D, 22 Sept)
Australia v Portugal (C, 1 Oct)

Stadium de Toulouse

Situated in the heart of Toulouse, this venue is one of the oldest at the tournament after originally being built for the FIFA World Cup all the way back in 1938. Visiting fans to that tournament then noticed the stadium's likeness to Wembley, the home of the England football team, and it was duly given the nickname "Mini Wembley". It has since become the home of French football side Toulouse FC, but also regularly hosts big matches for rugby team Stade Toulousain.

The France national rugby team also play here occasionally too, having first done so back in 1963, and they have recorded some famous wins at the venue – including two victories over the All Blacks.

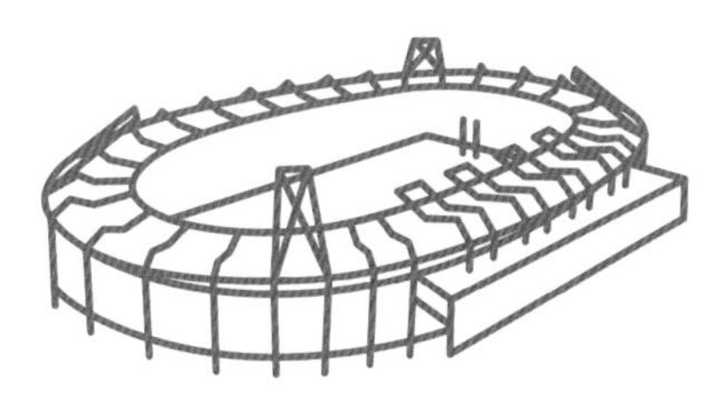

Location: .... Toulouse
Capacity: 33,103

The ground was renovated ahead of the FIFA World Cup in 1998, in which it played a prominent role, as it hosted six matches. It staged four games the last time Rugby World Cup was held in France in 2007, and it will do so again this time around, too.

MATCHES

Japan v Chile .... (D, 10 Sept)
New Zealand v Namibia ...... (A, 15 Sept)
Georgia v Portugal .... (C, 23 Sept)
Japan v Samoa .... (D, 28 Sept)
Fiji v Portugal .... (C, 8 Oct)

John Kirwan sparkles for New Zealand

22 May, 1987: Eden Park, Auckland

As co-hosts of the very first Rugby World Cup, the All Blacks wanted to lay down a marker in their opening game. They certainly did that against Italy, running out 70-6 winners, and winger John Kirwan was the star of the show. New Zealand had already scored 48 points when Kirwan produced a moment of magic that will live long in the memory. The All Blacks received the ball from kick-off and it quickly found its way to Kirwan. The wing was deep inside his own 22 when he got the ball, but that did not stop him as he took off. One by one, Kirwan side-stepped the Italy defence as he ran the length of the pitch to score under the posts.

Right: John Kirwan lit up the New Zealand team with his runs.

THE ROAD TO FRANCE

Just as the tournament is sure to itself, the road to Rugby World Cup 2023 has provided plenty of drama. After 12 teams qualified through their performances at the last tournament in Japan, there were eight more places up for grabs. As ever the competition was fierce, with sides desperate to be part of the greatest rugby show on earth. There were plenty of great stories along the way, but Chile stole the headlines as they reached their first-ever Rugby World Cup.

Left: Chile have made history by qualifying for their first-ever Rugby World Cup.

How the teams qualified

The Covid-19 pandemic made it a challenging situation for the qualification process of Rugby World Cup 2023, with much of rugby grinding to a halt in 2020. Once back up and running the following year, though, qualification began in earnest and it proved to be very competitive, with the culmination being the enthralling Final Qualification Tournament in 2022.

If Rugby World Cup 2019 taught us anything, it was that the game was becoming more competitive than ever.

The average winning margin between established and emerging unions decreased at the tournament in 2019, compared with 2015 benchmarks, and that all pointed to the qualification process for France being even tougher than before.

As the Covid-19 pandemic gripped the world in 2020, much of rugby stopped, but plans were put in place for 2021. The road to France would truly begin then, and World Rugby Chairman Sir Bill Beaumont declared how confirmation of the global qualification process for Rugby World Cup 2023 provided "a beacon of excitement" for everyone.

There were 12 teams who had already secured their places in France, with the top three finishers from the pools at Rugby World Cup 2019 automatically qualifying.

One of those was Fiji, and that left it to Samoa and Tonga to compete over a two-legged play-off to become Oceania's qualifier for the tournament in France.

Samoa proved to have too much for Tonga, winning 79-28 on aggregate over the two legs, and they became

Above: Samoa secured their place in France 2023 by beating Tonga in a two-legged play-off.

THE FINAL EIGHT'S ROAD TO QUALIFICATION

With 12 places at the tournament in France already secured by those teams who finished in the top three of their pools at Rugby World Cup 2019, eight places were left to be fought for.

THEY WERE DECIDED AS FOLLOWS:

Two European qualifiers, Europe 1 and 2: These were awarded to the teams that finished first and second in the combined Rugby Europe Championship 2021 and 2022 standings. Portugal progressed to the Final Qualification Tournament after coming third. **GEORGIA** and **ROMANIA**.

Two Americas qualifiers, Americas 1 and 2: The winner of the Rugby Americas North play-off, USA, faced the winner of the Sudamérica Rugby 3 Naciones, Uruguay, in a two-legged tie for a place in France. The runners-up of the Rugby Americas North play-off, Canada, and Sudamérica Rugby 3 Naciones, Chile, faced each other, with the winner then taking on the loser of USA v Uruguay in a two-legged tie for a place at Rugby World Cup 2023. USA lost and joined the Final Qualification Tournament. **URUGUAY** and **CHILE**.

One Oceania qualifier, Oceania 1: Samoa played Tonga over two legs in July 2021, with the winner claiming a spot in Pool D at Rugby World Cup 2023. **SAMOA**.

One Asia/Pacific qualifier, Asia/Pacific play-off: After losing to Samoa, Tonga beat the Cook Islands in the Asia/Pacific Qualifier. They then faced the winners of the Asia Rugby Championship 2022, Hong Kong, in a one-off winner-takes-all play-off for a place in France. Hong Kong lost and joined the Final Qualification Tournament. **TONGA**.

One African qualifier, Africa 1: The winners of the Rugby Africa Cup in 2022, which took place over two years, claimed a spot in France. Kenya, who lost in the final to Namibia, progressed to the Final Qualification Tournament. **NAMIBIA**.

Final Qualification Tournament winner: Four teams from across the world (Hong Kong, Kenya, Portugal and USA) were given one last chance to qualify for France. They played a round-robin tournament in Dubai in November 2022, with the winners securing the last spot at Rugby World Cup 2023. **PORTUGAL**.

Above: Tonga and Hong Kong played out a thrilling game in Australia, with Tonga qualifying.

the 13th team to book their place at Rugby World Cup 2023.

That would not be the end of Tonga's journey, though, and after beating the Cook Islands they secured a showdown in 2022 with the winners of the Asia Rugby Championship, Hong Kong.

The two sides would face each other in a one-off winner-takes-all play-off in Australia, with the victor heading to Rugby World Cup 2023 and the loser to the Final Qualification Tournament.

Tonga came into the match at the Sunshine Coast Stadium on a run of six defeats in a row, while Hong Kong were dreaming of qualifying for their first-ever Rugby World Cup.

Their hopes were dashed, however, by a brilliant performance from Tonga captain Sonatane Takalua, who scored a hat-trick on the way to his side winning 44-22.

"I am lucky enough to get these three tries but it wasn't just me, it was a great effort from all the boys and it is a big relief to get the win," Takalua said afterwards. "Tongan supporters are always behind us wherever we go in the world and to get support like this behind us tonight was a big push for us."

Tonga players celebrated after their fine win, but Hong Kong had to dust themselves down and get ready for the Final Qualification Tournament.

Many had been expecting Samoa and Tonga to qualify for Rugby World Cup 2023, but elsewhere the Americas qualifiers provided plenty of shocks.

After beating Canada over two legs in the Rugby Americas North play-off, USA set up a showdown with Uruguay – who had won the Sudamérica Rugby 3 Naciones ahead of Chile and Brazil.

The two-legged play-off between USA and Uruguay was historic, as the two nations had never played for the Americas 1 spot before. USA went into the tie as favourites too as, in nine previous Rugby World Cup qualifiers against Uruguay, the South Americans had only won once – and that was back in 2002.

Uruguay had also not beaten USA away from home, and that continued as they lost the first leg 19-16. They swiftly put that behind them, however, and won the return fixture 34-15 to progress 50-34 on aggregate.

Uruguay were worthy winners in front of their fans in Montevideo, producing some excellent running rugby to qualify for their fifth Rugby World Cup and third in a row. Emotional scenes followed at full-time, with players and fans breaking down in tears at the Estadio Charrúa.

Those scenes, however, were nothing compared to those in Chile. The South American side had already stunned Canada over two legs and their reward was a showdown with USA, who were looking to bounce back from defeat to Uruguay.

USA went into the matches as hot favourites, having won five of their six previous meetings against Chile and the last four by an average of more than 50 points. Chile, however, defied the odds and won two pulsating ties 52-51 on aggregate.

After losing the first leg at home 22-21, the South American side feared the worst. But Santiago Videla struck a late penalty during the second leg in Colorado to secure a 31-29 victory for Chile.

"It really means so much... there were times when it seemed like it was uphill," Chile captain Martín Sigren said, after his country qualified for their first Rugby World Cup. "I want to thank all the family who came here, they were the ones who kept us pushing."

USA's consolation would be that they could compete in the Final Qualification Tournament and they were joined there by Portugal, who had come third in the Rugby Europe Championship.

Above: Georgia impressed on their way to qualifying for another Rugby World Cup.

The results from that were taken over the course of 2021 and 2022, with Georgia impressing on their way to finishing top of the table.

Georgia were due to be joined by Spain in France, but World Rugby deemed they used an ineligible player during qualification. A 10-point penalty was applied to Spain and as such Romania qualified for Rugby World Cup 2023 instead, with Portugal promoted to third and heading to the Final Qualification Tournament.

The race to qualify from Africa had been taking place over two years and came to a conclusion in 2022, with Kenya and Namibia going head-to-head in Aix-en-Provence in France.

For Kenya, they were aiming to reach their first-ever Rugby World Cup, while Namibia were looking to qualify for the seventh time in a row.

In the end, Namibia put in a commanding performance to win 36-0, with flanker Wian Conradie scoring a hat-trick in the process.

Kenya's defeat meant that they entered the Final Qualification Tournament, as they, USA, Portugal and Hong Kong competed for the final place at Rugby World Cup 2023.

The four sides faced off in a round-robin tournament in Dubai, and it came down to the final game, as Portugal and USA both won their opening two matches.

Portugal went into the showdown with USA knowing a draw would be enough for them, as they topped the standings with a superior points difference.

What followed was a nervy contest, and Portugal were the victors as Samuel Marques kicked a penalty in the final seconds of the game. It secured a 16-16 draw for Portugal and prompted wild celebrations as they qualified for their first Rugby World Cup since 2007.

"It's hard to explain, it's one of the best feelings in the world," Portugal captain Tomás Appleton said. "For the rugby community this is amazing, we've been missing [from Rugby World Cups] for quite some time and we need a new generation to inspire the kids."

FINAL QUALIFICATION TOURNAMENT TABLE

Team	W	D	L	PF	PA	BP	Pts
Portugal	2	1	0	143	30	2	12
USA	2	1	0	133	37	2	12
Hong Kong	1	0	2	43	109	0	4
Kenya	0	0	3	32	175	1	1

Above: Portugal qualified for their first Rugby World Cup since 2007.

World Rugby Rankings

The competitive nature of the current rugby landscape can be summed up by the World Rugby Men's Rankings powered by Capgemini. During the course of 2022, three sides were ranked number one, and that only underlines how close the top teams are going into Rugby World Cup 2023. It will be all to play for when the sides meet in France.

There was a time when New Zealand were an unstoppable force at the top of the World Rugby Men's Rankings powered by Capgemini.

Until August 2019, they had reigned supreme as the number one team in the world for a staggering 509 weeks in a row after winning two Rugby World Cups on the spin. That incredible run was halted by Wales overtaking them in top spot and, since then, the battle to be the best team in the world has been more competitive than ever.

That was certainly the case during 2022, with three sides all enjoying time as the number one team in the world. South Africa started the year in top spot, with New Zealand behind them and England sitting in third. Trailing just behind them were Ireland and France, but it would not be long before those two sides were looking down on the rest.

France enjoyed a brilliant Six Nations, winning the Grand Slam, and, by March, they had climbed to second, with their eyes firmly on top spot. They eventually

Above: Ireland enjoyed a fine 2022, finishing it as the number one ranked team in the world.

HOW THEY WORK

The World Rugby Men's Rankings powered by Capgemini have been in place since 2003 and are calculated using a 'Points Exchange' system, whereby one side takes points off another based on the match result.

All countries have a rating, typically between 0 and 100, with the number one side usually over 90.

The point exchanges are based on the match result, the relative strength of each team, and the margin of victory, and there is also an allowance for home advantage.

Points exchanges are doubled during a Rugby World Cup to recognise the importance of the event, but all other full international matches are treated the same.

Above: Argentina are proof of how nations can go from emerging sides into top-10 teams.

achieved that aim in July, becoming the number one team in the world for the first time in their history after beating Japan, and New Zealand lost to Ireland.

Their time at the top, however, lasted just a week and summed up how close the best teams in the world are right now. New Zealand's reign of dominance is over and fittingly Ireland leapfrogged France by beating the All Blacks 32-22.

It was an historic moment for Ireland, who have been top of the World Rugby Men's Rankings powered by Capgemini before – but never had they broken through the 90-point barrier since the rankings were introduced in October 2003. A strong series of results in November meant Ireland kept their place as the number one team at the end of 2022.

It has been a rollercoaster year for many sides, such as Australia. The Wallabies started the Autumn Nations Series in ninth place, but finished it in sixth after wins against Scotland and Wales.

New Zealand also endured a turbulent 12 months and twice during the Rugby Championship they slipped to an historic low of fifth in the rankings. They bounced back to win the title, climbing to fourth in the process, and they will be determined to be back on top spot by the end of 2023.

It was a more memorable year for Chile, who qualified for their first-ever Rugby World Cup and reached a new record ranking of 21st.

There was plenty of movement elsewhere in the World Rugby Men's Rankings powered by Capgemini during 2022, as many of the emerging nations looked to climb the ladder to the top.

It is tight at the top of the rankings, but the same applies lower down, and teams enjoyed some huge climbs at various times.

Lithuania, for example, moved up nine places to 39th in November, while the likes of Serbia and Switzerland enjoyed eight-place jumps earlier on in the year.

WORLD RUGBY RANKINGS – TOP 50

(as at 1st March 2023)

Position	*Team*	*Points*
1	IRELAND	91.33
2	FRANCE	89.47
3	NEW ZEALAND	88.98
4	SOUTH AFRICA	88.97
5	SCOTLAND	83.26
6	ENGLAND	83.11
7	AUSTRALIA	81.80
8	ARGENTINA	80.72
9	JAPAN	77.39
10	WALES	76.88
11	SAMOA	76.03
12	GEORGIA	75.94
13	ITALY	75.83
14	FIJI	74.84
15	TONGA	71.21
16	PORTUGAL	66.94
17	SPAIN	66.42
18	URUGUAY	66.24
19	USA	65.92
20	ROMANIA	64.45
21	NAMIBIA	61.60
22	CHILE	60.89
23	CANADA	60.46
24	HONG KONG	59.66
25	RUSSIA	58.06
26	BRAZIL	55.23
27	BELGIUM	54.41
28	NETHERLANDS	54.39
29	POLAND	53.96
30	SWITZERLAND	53.80
31	KOREA	52.62
32	ZIMBABWE	52.43
33	KENYA	51.79
34	GERMANY	51.52
35	CZECHIA	50.26
36	UKRAINE	49.61
37	COLOMBIA	48.69
38	TUNISIA	48.55
39	PARAGUAY	48.14
40	LITHUANIA	48.09
41	SWEDEN	48.06
42	PHILIPPINES	47.80
43	UGANDA	47.25
44	MADAGASCAR	46.89
45	MALTA	46.75
46	SRI LANKA	46.73
47	CROATIA	46.67
48	MOROCCO	46.33
49	IVORY COAST	46.24
50	MALAYSIA	46.12

16

RUGBY
WORLD CUP
FRANCE 2023

MEET THE TEAMS

Reigning champions South Africa will be looking to retain their crown in France, but they face plenty of stiff competition from a number of teams. New Zealand are eyeing a fourth Rugby World Cup triumph, while France are in high spirits as hosts. Emerging nations are looking to make their mark on the biggest stage too, and Chile are making their first-ever appearance at a Rugby World Cup after impressing during qualification for the tournament.

Left: England have appeared at every Rugby World Cup, winning it back in 2003.

New Zealand

After missing out on becoming world champions for a third time in a row back at Rugby World Cup 2019, New Zealand are hungry to regain their crown this time around in France. For so long the dominant force on the rugby planet, the All Blacks are determined to be on top of the world again.

Above: New Zealand beat neighbours Australia to take the 2015 crown.

New Zealand head to Rugby World Cup 2023 with a point to prove and eager to banish the painful memories they have from the last tournament in France. That was back in 2007, and the All Blacks had been tipped as many people's favourites to go all the way that year. They looked on course to do so as well during the pool stage, which they cruised through, winning all four of their matches and scoring on average more than 75 points a game.

However, the All Blacks were stunned by hosts France in the next round, as for the first time in their history they were knocked out at the quarter-final stage. New Zealand dominated large parts of the game, but they could not turn their dominance into points and in the end they were made to pay. France ran out 20-18 winners in Cardiff, with centre Yannick Jauzion the hero on the night.

Seemingly spurred on by that disappointment, New Zealand went on to win the next two Rugby World Cups as they enjoyed a golden era, with the likes of Dan Carter and Richie McCaw driving them on to be the leading team in the game.

At Rugby World Cup 2019, New Zealand had been aiming to be the first team to lift the Webb Ellis Cup three times in a row, and there will be plenty of regret that they did not ultimately achieve that feat. New Zealand beat eventual champions South Africa during the pool stage, finishing ahead of them, but they came unstuck in the semi-finals against

ALL BLACKS®

RWC STATS

Played: 56
Won: 49
Lost: 7
Drawn: 0
Winning percentage: 87.5%
Points for: 2,552
Points against: 753
Biggest victory: 145-17
v Japan in Bloemfontein
on 4 June, 1995
Heaviest defeat: 22-10
v Australia in Sydney
on 15 November, 2003
World Rugby Men's Rankings powered by Capgemini: 3

COACH

IAN FOSTER

Part of the New Zealand setup since 2011, Ian Foster was given the head coach job in December 2019 after Steve Hansen departed. They were big shoes for Foster to fill, with Hansen guiding the All Blacks to Rugby World Cup triumph in 2015. Foster, however, played his role in that victory as an assistant. His reign as New Zealand head coach endured a rocky time in 2022, resulting in members of his backroom staff being replaced.

STAR PLAYER

ARDIE SAVEA

Position: .... Back-row
Born: ....14 October, 1993, Wellington, New Zealand
Club: .... Hurricanes (NZL)
Height: 1.90m (6ft 3in)
Weight: 99kg (15st 8lb)
Caps: 70
Points: ....100 (20 tries)

Since making his New Zealand debut in 2016, Ardie Savea has gone on to establish himself as one of the best back-row forwards in the world. When it comes to pace and power, there are few players who can match the All Black and he is one of the most dynamic players on the planet – with and without the ball. Savea is from a proud rugby family, with his brother, Julian, also representing the All Blacks. Savea's performances in 2019 saw him nominated for World Rugby Men's 15s Player of the Year, and in 2021 he was crowned the All Blacks' player of the year.

a formidable England team. It was the All Blacks' first loss at a Rugby World Cup for a staggering 12 years, while it was also only their second defeat to England in their previous 17 encounters against them.

Semi-final exits, like the one in 2019, used to be a common occurrence for the All Blacks who, after winning the inaugural Rugby World Cup in 1987, struggled to retain their crown. In 1991, 1999 and 2003 they suffered semi-final defeats as the strength in depth among the world's rugby nations was proven.

Given the talent available to them, New Zealand should have arguably won more than the three Rugby World Cups they have claimed so far. Of all their near-misses, defeat in the final of the 1995 tournament perhaps stings the most. That side was blessed with the legendary wing Jonah Lomu, whose pace and power made him an unstoppable force. He finished the tournament with seven tries, the joint-most of any player, but New Zealand as a team left empty-handed as hosts South Africa pipped them in the final.

Now back in France, the scene of their worst-ever Rugby World Cup performance, New Zealand will be determined to be champions once again. It has not been plain sailing since 2019, though, even if the All Blacks won the Rugby Championship in 2021 and 2022. In 2022 they suffered their first-ever home loss to Argentina, slipping to number five in the World Rugby Men's Rankings powered by Capgemini – their lowest ever position. The defeat was also New Zealand's fourth loss of the year – unheard of by their high standards – and it led some to question the credentials of the current side. History has shown us, though, that we should never write off the All Blacks.

RUGBY WORLD CUP PERFORMANCES

1987 .... CHAMPIONS
1991 .... Third
1995 .... Runners-up
1999 .... Fourth
2003 .... Third
2007 .... Quarter-final
2011 .... CHAMPIONS
2015 .... CHAMPIONS
2019 .... Third

POOL A

France

France have never won a Rugby World Cup, but they will be dreaming that now is the moment to finally end that long wait. They have reached the final of three previous tournaments, but always come unstuck when they have been in touching distance of glory. The support of a home crowd could help them get over that last hurdle.

Above: France have come so close to glory on three occasions, such as in 2011.

Given the number of talented players who have pulled on the famous blue jersey of France, it is one of rugby's great mysteries that they have never won a Rugby World Cup.

That talent was evident from the very first tournament all the way back in 1987. It was there that Les Bleus showed the world what they can do, with full-back Serge Blanco's try against Australia going down as one of the greatest in history. That moment of magic booked France a place in the final against New Zealand, but they were defeated by the All Blacks and since then it has been a series of near-misses for the men in blue. Their flamboyant flair, however, has never faded and instead been associated with France ever since, even if the trophies this rugby nation deserves have not always followed.

At Rugby World Cup 1991, France crashed out at the quarter-final stage, and then during the next four tournaments they just came up short. They reached three semi-finals, as well as the final of Rugby World Cup 1999, but Les Bleus just could not end their wait to lift the Webb Ellis Cup. During that time they still continued to entertain, with the likes of fly-half Frédéric Michalak playing with the type of freedom that made France such a joy to watch at times.

No more so was that the case than at Rugby World Cup 2007, when France pulled off one of the great shocks to beat New Zealand in the quarter-finals. Frustratingly, however,

FRANCE RUGBY

RWC STATS

Played: 52
Won: 36
Lost: 15
Drawn: 1
Winning percentage: 69.2%
Points for: 1,588
Points against: 996
Biggest victory: 87-10 v Namibia in Toulouse on 16 September, 2007
Heaviest defeat: 62-13 v New Zealand in Cardiff on 17 October, 2015
World Rugby Men's Rankings powered by Capgemini: 2

COACH

FABIEN GALTHIÉ

After enjoying an impressive playing career, where he captained France at Rugby World Cup 2003, Fabien Galthié moved into working as a coach. He initially worked in the French club rugby scene but came onboard the national team as an assistant to Jacques Brunel, with the plan being he would replace him the following year. Galthié has proven to be a bold head coach, opting to play exciting rugby and blood youngsters at the same time.

STAR PLAYER

GRÉGORY ALLDRITT

Position: .... Number eight
Born: .... 23 March, 1997, Condom-en-Armagnac, France
Club: .... Stade Rochelais (FRA)
Height: 1.91m (6ft 3in)
Weight: 115kg (18st 1lb)
Caps: 37
Points: .... 20 (4 tries)

Grégory Alldritt had only just come onto the international scene when he was picked to be part of the France squad for the last Rugby World Cup. The forward has come on leaps and bounds since then, and he is without doubt one of the best number eights on the planet. Understandably Alldritt's ability to carry the ball and break through tackles catches the eye, but his awareness to offload in contact is what really makes him so dangerous. He is also a brilliant defender and often tops the charts when it comes to the most turnovers in a match.

their dream of going all the way as hosts was then ended by England in the very next round.

However, at Rugby World Cup 2011 Les Bleus took a different tack and became renowned for their defence and discipline. Led by the exceptional Thierry Dusautoir, they stunned England in the quarter-finals and then sneaked past Wales to reach the final. Their new resolve had fans thinking this was the moment they would finally become world champions, but a painful 8-7 loss to host New Zealand dashed their hopes.

It was widely believed that France could build off being runners-up in 2011, but their last two tournaments have been disappointing. Two successive quarter-final exits is their worst ever run and it was no surprise that, after Rugby World Cup 2019, France opted to do a reboot of their team. The decision was taken to revamp the squad and blood young players, with the idea being that they would be ready to lead the country to glory by the time 2023 rolled around. Indeed, in 2020, ahead of that year's Six Nations, head coach Fabien Galthié named 19 uncapped players in his squad.

Many of those called upon were stars from France's under-20 side, who had impressed at that level, and now the likes of Cameron Woki and Romain Ntamack are thriving on the senior stage. Led by the supremely talented scrum-half Antoine Dupont, France's young stars swept all before them to win the Six Nations Grand Slam in 2022. Their final win of that triumph was a victory over England in Paris, where a raucous Stade de France roared the home team on to glory.

France seemingly have their swagger back and, finally, it feels like their long wait to be world champions could end on home soil.

RUGBY WORLD CUP PERFORMANCES

1987 ....Runners-up
1991 ....Quarter-final
1995 ....Third
1999 ....Runners-up
2003 ....Fourth
2007 ....Fourth
2011 ....Runners-up
2015 ....Quarter-final
2019 ....Quarter-final

Italy

A regular fixture at every Rugby World Cup to date, Italy are still waiting to make their first appearance in the quarter-finals. They have threatened to do so on more than one ocassion in the past, but face a tall order this time around after being drawn in a pool with New Zealand and France.

Above: Italy cemented their place at the top of their pool with this win over Canada in 2019.

In many ways Italy's Rugby World Cup history can be summed up by their performance at the very first tournament. Back then, in 1987, Italy were on the cusp of reaching the quarter-finals after they, Argentina and Fiji all earned one win from a pool that also contained eventual champions New Zealand. Sadly for Italy, Fiji took the spot in the knockout stages having scored more tries. Ever since then, Italy have been banging on the door of the quarter-finals and they are determined to make history in France.

Since the turn of the millennium, the country has made progress after they were added into the Six Nations. That innovation came at a vital time for Italy, as they had just come off the back of a disappointing showing at Rugby World Cup 1999, where they failed to win a single match. Something had to change and, by being added to the Six Nations, they were given the chance to test themselves against some of the best rugby teams on earth. It felt like a new dawn for Italy and there have been some brilliant moments – not least their first-ever victory over current world champions South Africa in 2016. "Today we rode the rollercoaster and we survived by sheer heart and courage," said the then Italy head coach Conor O'Shea. "They weren't just brave, they were heroic."

Italy have become consistent performers at Rugby World Cups, regularly winning two of their pool

RWC STATS

Played: 31
Won: 13
Lost: 18
Drawn: 0
Winning percentage: 41.9%
Points for: 627
Points against: 977
Biggest victory: 48-7
v Canada in Fukuoka
on 26 September, 2019
Heaviest defeat: 101-3
v New Zealand in Huddersfield
on 14 October, 1999
World Rugby Men's Rankings powered by Capgemini: 13

COACH

KIERAN CROWLEY

Appointed as Italy's head coach in May 2021, Kieran Crowley has worked hard to transform the team. He has plenty of experience in Italian rugby, after spending five years working in the country coaching club side Benetton. Crowley has also previously been in charge at international level after working with Canada. During his playing career, Crowley played for New Zealand and was part of the squad that won the inaugural Rugby World Cup back in 1987.

STAR PLAYER

MICHELE LAMARO

Position: .... Flanker
Born: .... 3 June, 1998, Rome, Italy
Club: .... Benetton (ITA)
Height: 1.88m (6ft 2in)
Weight: 103kg (16st 3lb)
Caps: 24
Points: 0

Italy have a rich history of producing back-row forwards and Michele Lamaro is the latest star to be making headlines. Despite him being only 23 at the time, head coach Kieran Crowley opted to make Lamaro captain in 2021, and he has thrived in a new leadership role. Lamaro can carry the ball well, but what makes him stand out is his ability in defence, after idolising New Zealand legend Richie McCaw and emulating his style. No one made more tackles than Lamaro during the 2022 Six Nations and he typifies the fighting spirit this new Italian team has under Crowley.

matches, but they have often fallen short in their crunch pool game. Frustratingly for them, in Japan in 2019 that was taken out of their hands as their final match with New Zealand was cancelled due to a typhoon hitting the country. Many will argue that victory would have been unlikely for Italy against the All Blacks, who they have never beaten, but the fact that it was taken out of their hands was hard to take.

Since Rugby World Cup 2019, just as in 2000, it feels like another dawn is taking place within Italian rugby and they are heading into a new era. They have often been a physical side, who have used their powerful forwards to compete with more established rugby nations, but under head coach Kieran Crowley they have become more expansive in their play.

Young backs such as Ange Capuozzo have added a flair to Italy's play, and that much was clear during the 2022 Six Nations. Italy were under huge pressure going into their final match of the tournament, as they had not won a game in the championship for seven years. Facing Wales in a packed stadium in Cardiff, few people gave them a chance, but they rose to the occasion in style. Edoardo Padovani scored a last-minute try after Capuozzo's brilliant break, and then another youngster, Paolo Garbisi, slotted the conversion to give Italy a 22-21 win.

"There was a lot of emotion, Marius Goosen our defence coach has been there six years and won his first Six Nations game, you would think we had won the World Cup," said Crowley.

Suddenly, the future feels bright for Italy once again and hope has been restored to a nation dreaming of success in France at Rugby World Cup 2023.

RUGBY WORLD CUP PERFORMANCES

1987 .... Pool stage
1991 .... Pool stage
1995 .... Pool stage
1999 .... Pool stage
2003 .... Pool stage
2007 .... Pool stage
2011 .... Pool stage
2015 .... Pool stage
2019 .... Pool stage

URU

Uruguay

Rugby World Cup 2023 will be Uruguay's fifth tournament, and morale is high. They defeated the USA to qualify via the Americas 1 play-off and now they will be out to build on that in France. Uruguay have never won more than one game at a tournament, but there is belief that can change.

Above: Uruguay pulled off one of the great Rugby World Cup shocks by beating Fiji in 2019.

If you want to know what playing and winning at a Rugby World Cup means to Uruguay, then you need only look back at Juan Manuel Gaminara in 2019.

Uruguay had gone into that tournament in Japan looking for a first Rugby World Cup win in 16 years and the odds looked against them when they faced Fiji in their opening match.

What followed, however, was a performance full of heart and passion as Uruguay claimed an historic 30-27 victory. It was a major shock – one that was celebrated wildly back in Uruguay – and Gaminara could not contain his emotions afterwards: "We've been preparing for this for four years so I'm really proud," he said.

Gaminara's words summed up Uruguay's spirit and, for a country with a population of around 3.5 million, they continually punch above their weight.

That was certainly the case back in 1999, when Uruguay were competing in their first-ever Rugby World Cup. Rugby may have been in the professional era then, but they were still an amateur side and they headed to the tournament with many writing them off.

Despite that, they claimed a victory over Spain and, just like Gaminara in 2019, their coach back then, Daniel Herrera, was emotional.

"It's like being world champions," he said. "It's almost a miracle for a country like ours to be here."

Uruguay made it to Rugby World Cup 2003 and recorded another victory, this time over Georgia. A heavy defeat to England, though, in which they

RWC STATS

Played: 15
Won: 3
Lost: 12
Drawn: 0
Winning percentage: 20%
Points for: 188
Points against: 718
Biggest victory: 27-15 v Spain in Galashiels on 2 October, 1999
Heaviest defeat: 111-13 v England in Brisbane on 2 November, 2003
World Rugby Men's Rankings powered by Capgemini: 18

COACH

ESTEBAN MENESES

Appointed in December 2015 after Pablo Lemoine stepped down, Esteban Meneses has impressed in his first international coaching job. He has guided Uruguay to successive Rugby World Cups and at the 2019 tournament they recorded an historic victory over Fiji. They qualified well for this tournament in France, beating USA over two legs in October 2021. It was the first time in their history that Uruguay had qualified for a Rugby World Cup as the Americas 1 team.

STAR PLAYER

ANDRÉS VILASECA

Position: ....Centre
Born: ....8 May, 1991, Montevideo, Uruguay
Club: ....Vannes (FRA)
Height: 1.85m (6ft 1in)
Weight: 96kg (15st 2lb)
Caps: 64
Points: ....74 (11 tries)

Andrés Vilaseca is a testament to the growth of rugby in Uruguay and evidence of how they are establishing themselves. He began his career playing club rugby in Uruguay, but since then he has broadened his horizons. Vilaseca has played in the USA and most recently he secured a move to French club Vannes. The centre earned that move after his fine performances for Uruguay, of whom he has been captain since the last Rugby World Cup. First capped by Uruguay in 2013, Vilaseca is the only Uruguay player to have played in every game at the last two Rugby World Cups.

conceded more than 100 points, was a reminder of the work that still needed to be done.

After missing out on the next two tournaments, Uruguay qualified for Rugby World Cup 2015, but for the first time in their history they failed to win a game.

Great strides were made after that, though, and increased investment has helped the team, as well. They now have a High Performance Centre in Montevideo and the current crop of players are proof of the benefits of that.

Uruguay have come a long way from the amateur days of 1999 and their showing at Rugby World Cup 2019 underlined that fact. A historic victory over Fiji set the tone, and they gave good accounts of themselves in other games despite losing – particularly against Wales.

The challenge for Uruguay now is to keep their trajectory on an upward curve. Under head coach Esteban Meneses they have been making strides and their qualifying performance for Rugby World Cup 2023 was their best ever, as they beat USA in a two-legged play-off to qualify as Americas 1.

The wider world is taking notice of Uruguay's growth and they are benefiting from players going abroad to play their club rugby. A number of the current crop – such as fly-half Felipe Berchesi and scrum-half Santiago Arata – play in France, and that has improved their game.

The team is evolving, too. Uruguay have always been a physical side, full of heart and passion, but they are adding style to go with their substance.

The dream for Rugby World Cup 2023 is to leave the tournament having won two matches. It will be a tall order, but Uruguay love nothing more than a challenge and proving people wrong.

RUGBY WORLD CUP PERFORMANCES

1987 .... Did not play
1991 .... Did not play
1995 .... Did not qualify
1999 .... Pool stage
2003 .... Pool stage
2007 .... Did not qualify
2011 .... Did not qualify
2015 .... Pool stage
2019 .... Pool stage

Namibia

Rugby World Cup 2023 will be Namibia's seventh tournament in a row and they are determined to make it one to remember. They are still yet to win a Rugby World Cup match, but they have come incredibly close to doing so over the years. Under experienced head coach Allister Coetzee, there is real belief the wait could finally be over.

Above: Namibia have appeared in every Rugby World Cup since 1999.

For Namibia, Rugby World Cup 2019 was another steep learning curve as they continue to develop their game.

It is easy to forget that this is a country that did not gain independence until three years after the very first Rugby World Cup in 1987 and, as such, Namibia are still in the infancy of their rugby career.

They have qualified for every Rugby World Cup since 1999, but still they are waiting for a first-ever win at the tournament. The hope was that would come in Japan in 2019, and Namibia started well in their opening game against Italy, taking the lead through Damian Stevens and holding their own.

Italy eventually ran away to a 47-22 victory in the second half and after that Namibia suffered two defeats at the hands of New Zealand (the then reigning world champions) and South Africa (the eventual winners in Japan).

Namibia's match against fellow emerging nation Canada was then cancelled due to Typhoon Hagibis and, as a result, Namibia's search for a Rugby World Cup win goes on.

Namibia have certainly come a long way since their first tournament in 1999, though, where they in fact were beaten 72-11 by Canada. Four years later, things were worse, as they conceded more than 300 points in four pool defeats. One of those was a 142-0 loss against hosts Australia and the defeat served as a low point from which Namibia have built upwards.

By Rugby World Cup 2007, the mentality of the team had changed.

RWC STATS

Played: 22
Won: 0
Lost: 22
Drawn: 0
Winning percentage: 0%
Points for: 248
Points against: 1,323
Biggest victory: N/A
Heaviest defeat: 142-0 v Australia in Adelaide on 25 October, 2003
World Rugby Men's Rankings powered by Capgemini: 21

COACH

ALLISTER COETZEE

Having worked in coaching for more than 25 years, Allister Coetzee has a wealth of experience. He was part of the coaching staff that helped South Africa win Rugby World Cup 2007 and he landed the Springboks' top job in 2016. Coetzee lost his job in charge of South Africa two years later, but he is back on the international stage with Namibia and has impressed after guiding them to qualification for Rugby World Cup 2023.

STAR PLAYER

JOHAN DEYSEL

Position: .... Centre
Born: .... 26 September, 1991, Windhoek, Namibia
Club: .... Union sportive Colomiers Rugby (FRA)
Height: 1.84m (6ft)
Weight: 93kg (14st 9lb)
Caps: 32
Points: .... 60 (12 tries)

A veteran of two Rugby World Cups, Johan Deysel now has the honour of captaining his country as they head to France. The 31-year-old plays his club rugby there for Union sportive Colomiers Rugby, but before that he spent his career playing in South Africa. Deysel is a strong and powerful centre in both attack and defence. No more so was that evident than at Rugby World Cup 2015, where Deysel shot to fame for his try against New Zealand. Receiving the ball near the line, Deysel got past two defenders before bouncing off a third on his way to scoring.

During that record loss to Australia in 2003, Namibia had been exposed defensively and they made sure that would no longer be the case.

The emergence of flanker Jacques Burger summed up their fighting spirit and dogged defence, and at Rugby World Cup 2007 they suffered a respectable 32-17 loss to Ireland.

In 2011, Namibia had to cope with being drawn in the "Pool of Death" with South Africa, Wales, Samoa and Fiji. That resulted in some heavy losses, but they did push Fiji all the way and scored 25 points in defeat to them.

Rugby World Cup 2015 turned out to be their most competitive yet as, for the first time, they scored against New Zealand during a 58-14 loss.

"I can remember every second like it was yesterday. I don't think I will ever forget it," try scorer Johan Deysel told World Rugby. "It is my best rugby memory."

Namibia went on to lose to Tonga 35-21 and then, most cruelly of all, they lost 17-16 to Georgia when a first-ever Rugby World Cup win had looked likely.

Namibia continue to make strides as an emerging rugby nation and they impressed during qualification for Rugby World Cup 2023.

A 36-0 victory in the final of the Rugby Africa Cup 2022 against Kenya underlined their development and the players celebrated wildly at full-time.

Under head coach Allister Coetzee there has been clear progress and that is unsurprising given the South African's vast experience.

Having been part of the Springboks coaching staff that won Rugby World Cup 2007, Coetzee knows what it takes to win at a tournament.

Namibia showed in qualifying that they have improved, but now they want to make their mark on the biggest stage of all in France.

RUGBY WORLD CUP PERFORMANCES

1987 .... Did not play
1991 .... Did not qualify
1995 .... Did not qualify
1999 .... Pool stage
2003 .... Pool stage
2007 .... Pool stage
2011 .... Pool stage
2015 .... Pool stage
2019 .... Pool stage

Wales stunned by Western Samoa

6 October, 1991: Cardiff Arms Park, Cardiff

Over the years there have been plenty of shocks and upsets at Rugby World Cups, but Western Samoa's win over Wales in 1991 was one of the first. Playing at their first-ever Rugby World Cup, little was known of or expected from Western Samoa, who it was estimated had only around 2,000 players to pick from. The island nation, however, more than punched above their weight as they beat Wales in their own backyard. They were worthy winners too, with Western Samoa's brilliant defence key to them toppling Wales. To'o Vaega and Sila Vaifale were the heroes on the day as they scored tries, but this was very much a team performance and proof that anyone can win on their day at a Rugby World Cup.

Right: Western Samoa stun Wales in Cardiff.

South Africa

When it comes to Rugby World Cups, no one has a knack of delivering when the time is right more than South Africa. The Springboks have lifted the famous Webb Ellis Cup on three occasions and they head to France as reigning champions – and undoubtedly one of the favourites to go all the way again.

Above: South Africa captain Siya Kolisi holding the Webb Ellis Cup has become an iconic image.

Before the last Rugby World Cup, despite their famous history, South Africa were very much flying under the radar. The Springboks had sacked their head coach Allister Coetzee just over a year out from the tournament and Rassie Erasmus was tasked with taking the reins. "It's a huge task to coach the Springboks," he said in March 2018. "I really believe we have the players and the rugby to turn things around and to mount a serious challenge at the Rugby World Cup."

Erasmus turned out to be a man of his word and South Africa went all the way in Japan, with performances reminiscent of their great sides of the past. Their physicality could not be matched by other teams and the sight of Siya Kolisi lifting the trophy aloft in Tokyo will go down in the history books.

Kolisi's journey is a remarkable one, with the flanker growing up in the impoverished township of Zwide, just outside Port Elizabeth. Despite his humble beginnings, Kolisi rose up to lead South Africa to glory in 2019 and the sight of him holding the Webb Ellis Cup brought back memories of Rugby World Cup 1995. That was South Africa's first appearance at the tournament and, as hosts, they were crowned champions. Their performance united the nation, with president Nelson Mandela iconically wearing the famous Springbok jersey with number six on the back as he handed captain Francois Pienaar the trophy. Just 24 years on, this time it

RWC STATS

Played:	43
Won:	36
Lost:	7
Drawn:	0
Winning percentage:	83.7%
Points for:	1,512
Points against:	553
Biggest victory:	87-0 v Namibia in Auckland on 22 September, 2011
Heaviest defeat:	29-9 v New Zealand in Melbourne on 8 November, 2003
World Rugby Men's Rankings powered by Capgemini:	4

COACH

JACQUES NIENABER

After Rassie Erasmus guided South Africa to Rugby World Cup glory in 2019, it was speculated if he would stay on in the role. In 2020, however, he moved back to his role as director of rugby and Jacques Nienaber was made head coach. Nienaber had previously been an assistant and knows the Springbok setup well as a result, but this is the first time he has ever taken on the role of head coach.

STAR PLAYER

SIYA KOLISI

Position: .... Flanker
Born: .... 16 June, 1991, Zwide, South Africa
Club: .... Sharks (RSA)
Height: 1.87m (6ft 2in)
Weight: 106kg (16st 9lb)
Caps: 75
Points: .... 45 (9 tries)

Siya Kolisi is someone who transcends rugby and his wider significance cannot be overlooked. The first black man to captain the Springboks, he led them to Rugby World Cup glory in 2019 and he has become a hero in South Africa. Kolisi very much leads by example and his ferocity in the tackle makes him one of the best defenders on the planet. Despite suffering with a bout of Covid-19, Kolisi was in formidable form in 2021 and he was duly crowned South African Rugby Player of the Year. He will be key to South Africa's hopes in France.

was Kolisi wearing the number six jersey as he held the trophy up to the Tokyo sky. That demonstrates the power of rugby in South Africa and their performances at Rugby World Cups are very impressive.

After the triumph in 1995, South Africa made the semi-finals in 1999 and then the quarter-finals in 2003, when England went all the way. After the disappointment of 2003, South Africa roared back in style at Rugby World Cup 2007 as they were once again crowned world champions. That South Africa team boasted some incredible forwards, including the likes of captain John Smit, second-row Victor Matfield and flanker Schalk Burger. In the backs, they had legendary centre Jean de Villiers and flying wing Bryan Habana, while the boot of Percy Montgomery meant they always had the scoreboard ticking over. After beating England 36-0 in their opening game, the Springboks never looked back on their way to lifting the Webb Ellis Cup. That march to victory happened in France and South Africa will have fond memories returning to the country this time around.

In many ways, their team now has some hallmarks of that great side from 2007. The Springbok pack is full of power, so much so that the forwards who come off the bench to close-out games have been dubbed 'The Bomb Squad' by the media. There is plenty of talent in the backs too, though, and with Faf de Klerk marshalling them from scrum-half they have the ability to blow teams away when they click. Just ask the British and Irish Lions side who lost their series there in 2021. That series victory over the Lions in 2021 has boosted confidence in South Africa and now they will have their sights set on retaining the Webb Ellis Cup for the first time in their history.

RUGBY WORLD CUP PERFORMANCES

1987 .... Did not play
1991 .... Did not play
1995 .... CHAMPIONS
1999 .... Third
2003 .... Quarter-final
2007 .... CHAMPIONS
2011 .... Quarter-final
2015 .... Third
2019 .... CHAMPIONS

Ireland

Despite over the years having teams blessed with plenty of talent, Ireland are still yet to make it past the quarter-finals of a Rugby World Cup. After so many painful defeats in the past, Ireland will be hoping this tournament in France is the moment they make history, with Andy Farrell now at the helm.

Above: Ireland reached the quarter-finals again at Rugby World Cup 2019.

After crashing out of Rugby World Cup 2019 at the quarter-final stage, the then Ireland captain Rory Best was crestfallen. It was the seventh time in nine attempts that Ireland had stumbled at that stage, as on this occasion a rampant New Zealand defeated them 46-14. "We've got a lot of big characters in that changing room and it's not often that you get deadly silence," Best said. "There were some of those big men in tears. That's what happens when everybody puts their heart and soul into something."

Pressure is a big factor in sport and it was clear from hearing Best speak that Ireland feel it whenever they reach the quarter-finals of a Rugby World Cup. It has become a major hurdle for them and, until they leap over it, that sense of doubt will hang over them. The frustrating thing for the men in green is that they so often look incredibly impressive during the pool stage of a Rugby World Cup.

In 2015, they won all of their pool games, beating France 24-9, but then they were blown away by Argentina in the quarter-finals. Four years earlier it was the same story, as once again Ireland had a 100 per cent record in the pool stage – only to then be undone by Wales in the knockout rounds.

Other than 2007, when Ireland failed to get out of their pool, and 1999, when they lost in the quarter-final play-off, it has always

RWC STATS

Played: 40
Won: 24
Lost: 16
Drawn: 0
Winning percentage: 60%
Points for: 1,108
Points against: 735
Biggest victory: 64-7 v Namibia in Sydney on 19 October, 2003
Heaviest defeat: 46-14 v New Zealand in Tokyo on 19 October, 2019
World Rugby Men's Rankings powered by Capgemini: 1

COACH

ANDY FARRELL

Previously an assistant with England and Ireland, Andy Farrell was given his chance to work as a head coach after Rugby World Cup 2019. Ireland had always planned for Farrell to take over from Joe Schmidt after the tournament and he has impressed in the top job. In 2022, he led Ireland to two wins over the All Blacks in New Zealand. That created history for Ireland, who had previously never beaten the All Blacks in New Zealand.

STAR PLAYER

JOHNNY SEXTON

Position: .... Fly-half
Born: .... 11 July, 1985, Dublin, Ireland
Club: .... Leinster (IRE)
Height: 1.88m (6ft 2in)
Weight: 90kg (14st 2lb)
Caps: .... 111 (+6 Lions)
Points: .... 1,034 (15 tries)

It is a sign of Johnny Sexton's incredible longevity that he was born before the very first Rugby World Cup in 1987 – and he is still going strong. Few players can boast a career like the fly-half and, whatever happens in France, he will go down as one of the game's greats. Sexton's ability to control a game makes him irreplaceable for Ireland and his ability to play so close to the gain-line makes him incredibly hard to defend against. Lethal with his boot too, the fly-half has scored more than 1,000 points for Ireland during his career.

been a case of the men in green failing at the final-eight stage. The hope is now, though, that under head coach Andy Farrell they can end that run and make it to at least the semi-finals.

There is certainly cause for plenty of optimism and Farrell has built on the fine work done by his predecessor, Joe Schmidt – who he worked under as an assistant. Before 2022, Ireland had never won a game against the All Blacks on New Zealand soil. But by the end of the year they had won two and claimed a series victory over them in the process. "Some of the stuff that they have done out there today, we have done it together so when you look at it like that I suppose it's the most proud that I've been as part of a group, without a shadow of a doubt," said Farrell.

The challenge for Ireland is to replicate that form at a Rugby World Cup, as it has been the case in the past that they have peaked outside of tournaments. Indeed, in the run-up to the last Rugby World Cup they beat New Zealand in 2016 and won the Six Nations Grand Slam in 2018, only to falter in Japan a year later.

This time around, with Farrell at the helm, Ireland are determined to make sure it is a different story after climbing to number one in the world rankings during 2022.

Their squad is packed with experience too, with the likes of captain Johnny Sexton hoping to put past Rugby World Cup disappointments behind him. Having made his debut for Ireland all the way back in 2009, Sexton has been there for plenty of lows at Rugby World Cups. Now, as he nears the end of his career, the fly-half will be hoping he is in France for a long overdue high.

RUGBY WORLD CUP PERFORMANCES

1987 .... Quarter-final
1991 .... Quarter-final
1995 .... Quarter-final
1999 .... Quarter-final play-off
2003 .... Quarter-final
2007 .... Pool stage
2011 .... Quarter-final
2015 .... Quarter-final
2019 .... Quarter-final

Scotland

Scotland have only once made it to the semi-finals of a Rugby World Cup and they are determined to try and change that record in France. Under head coach Gregor Townsend they have been rightly praised for their attractive style of rugby, but now the country is hungry for results to back it up.

Above: Scotland celebrate scoring in their quarter-final at Rugby World Cup 2015.

Given how much of a proud rugby nation Scotland are, it is difficult to comprehend how they have only made it to one Rugby World Cup semi-final.

They have come close on multiple occasions to repeating the feat they achieved in 1991, most notably when Australia beat them by a solitary point in the quarter-finals of Rugby World Cup 2015, but much of their history has been blighted by near-misses.

Scotland will hope that the long wait to return to the semi-finals ends in France, but they head there in the wake of two pool-stage exits in the previous three Rugby World Cups. The latest of those came in 2019, when Scotland finished third in Pool A behind hosts Japan and Ireland. They went into their final game against Japan with the threat of a typhoon calling the game off, but it eventually went ahead and they suffered a painful 28-21 loss to the hosts. "Experiences are what make you as a group and how you react to those experiences," said head coach Gregor Townsend. "We had the team and we had the ability at the start of that game to go on and win it by the necessary amount of points. That we did not is hugely disappointing. We have to learn from that."

That pool-stage exit was only the second one Scotland have experienced in their history, with the other coming back in 2011. On that occasion they finished third behind England and Argentina, but both losses were by the narrowest of margins. England

SCOTLAND

RWC STATS

Played: 42
Won: 24
Lost: 17
Drawn: 1
Winning percentage: ....57.1 per cent
Points for: 1,261
Points against: 803
Biggest victory: 89-0
v Ivory Coast in Rustenburg on 26 May, 1995
Heaviest defeat: 51-9
v France in Sydney on 25 October, 2003
World Rugby Men's Rankings powered by Capgemini: 5

COACH

GREGOR TOWNSEND

Having previously worked as head coach with Glasgow Warriors and attack coach at Scotland, Gregor Townsend landed the top job in 2017. Townsend has transformed the way Scotland play, encouraging them to be adventurous in attack. The change in style has been clear to see and Scotland have secured some big results, notably retaining the Calcutta Cup by beating England in 2021, 2022 and 2023. Townsend is now eyeing success at a Rugby World Cup.

STAR PLAYER

FINN RUSSELL

Position: .... Fly-half
Born: .... 23 September, 1992, Bridge of Allan, Scotland
Club: .... Racing 92 (FRA)
Height: 1.82m (6ft)
Weight: 87kg (13st 10lb)
Caps: .... 68 (+1 Lions)
Points: .... 287 (8 tries)

Finn Russell is undoubtedly one of the most exciting players to watch on the planet and he has the ability to win any game on his own. It was under current Scotland head coach, Gregor Townsend, that he initially shone, as he masterminded Glasgow Warriors to the PRO12 title in 2015. Since then, the fly-half has begun to flourish on the international stage and 2023 will be the third Rugby World Cup of his career. An ambitious and attacking player, Russell will have aspirations of firing Scotland to their second semi-final appearance in France this time around.

beat Scotland by four points and Argentina downed them by one.

The rest of Scotland's Rugby World Cup history has been a series of quarter-final exits and a solitary semi-final appearance, with New Zealand continually proving their nemesis. Indeed, in three of the first four tournaments, the All Blacks knocked them out at the quarter-final stage. Their one semi-final appearance came back in 1991 when, alongside England, France, Ireland and Wales, they were hosting the tournament. Scotland impressed during the pool stage, finishing on top of theirs and beating Ireland 24-15 in the process. That set up a quarter-final showdown with Western Samoa and once again they looked good, claiming a 28-6 win as John Jeffrey scored two tries.

Waiting in the semi-finals was England, and an expectant Murrayfield was dreaming of a victory over one of their great rivals. Defeat, however, came by the narrowest of margins as England squeezed past 9-6 in a low-scoring game, with Scotland's Gavin Hastings bemoaning the fact he missed a good shot at goal from close range.

Tight, cagey games like that have become a thing of the past for Scotland under Townsend who, since taking charge in 2017, has encouraged them to play attacking rugby. It has proved successful at times, with Scotland's approach certainly endearing themselves to supporters. The likes of Finn Russell and Stuart Hogg have shown themselves to be world-class players in that system and now they are determined to bounce back after their early exit at Rugby World Cup 2019.

The stage is set for Scotland, and Townsend's side will want to entertain on their way to victory.

RUGBY WORLD CUP PERFORMANCES

1987 .... Quarter-final
1991 .... Fourth
1995 .... Quarter-final
1999 .... Quarter-final
2003 .... Quarter-final
2007 .... Quarter-final
2011 .... Pool stage
2015 .... Quarter-final
2019 .... Pool stage

Tonga

Tonga have never made the knockout stages of a Rugby World Cup and they will be dreaming of ending that wait in France. A physical and powerful side, they have produced some memorable wins over the years and are capable of beating anyone on their day. A strong showing in France would underline how they are a team that is on the up.

Above: Tonga beat USA on their way to claiming two wins at Rugby World Cup 2007.

Both Fiji and Samoa have made the knockout stages of a Rugby World Cup and Tonga are determined to become the third Pacific Island nation to do so.

Over the years they have shown flashes of brilliance and claimed some big scalps, but maintaining that form over the course of a whole tournament has proved elusive.

The hope is that that can change in France and their head coach Toutai Kefu insists they are not there to simply make up the numbers.

"We are not happy with just attending Rugby World Cup. We want more. We want to win one or two pool games and go further," Kefu said after Tonga secured qualification by beating Hong Kong in 2022.

Tonga have certainly come a long way since they made their Rugby World Cup debut all the way back in 1987. They finished bottom of their pool then, failing to win a game, but there were signs of promise during a spirited 29-16 loss to Wales.

Tonga failed to qualify for the next tournament in 1991, but they returned four years later to claim their first-ever Rugby World Cup win. They beat Ivory Coast, although the match was overshadowed by an injury to the Ivory Coast's Max Brito, which left him paralysed.

After claiming their first win in tournament history, Tonga built on it at Rugby World Cup 1999 by claiming a famous victory over Italy. They edged a tight game 28-25 and

RWC STATS

Played: 29
Won: 8
Lost: 21
Drawn: 0
Winning percentage: 28%
Points for: 472
Points against: 966
Biggest victory: 29-11 v Ivory Coast in Rustenburg on 3 June, 1995
Heaviest defeat: 101-10 v England at Twickenham on 15 October, 1999
World Rugby Men's Rankings powered by Capgemini: 15

COACH

TOUTAI KEFU

After a glittering playing career, during which he won Rugby World Cup with Australia in 1999, Toutai Kefu is now looking to make his name as a coach. Appointed by Tonga in 2016, he has guided them to back-to-back Rugby World Cups. As a player, Kefu was revered for his quick and powerful play and he has looked to instil the same qualities in his team as he makes his mark in the coaching world.

STAR PLAYER

SONATANE TAKULUA

Position: .... Scrum-half
Born: .... 11 January, 1991, Tofoa, Tonga
Club: .... Sporting Union Agen Lot-et-Garonne (FRA)
Height: 1.76m (5ft 9in)
Weight: 101kg (15st 13lb)
Caps: 48
Points: .... 252 (14 tries)

Sonatane Takulua has been a key player for Tonga ever since he made his debut for them back in 2014. The scrum-half is Tonga's prime playmaker and his ability to score and make tries means he has the potential to shine at this Rugby World Cup. Takulua was a star for Tonga during qualification and he put in a captain's performance by scoring three tries in the Asia/Pacific 1 play-off against Hong Kong. The scrum-half has impressed at club level too, enjoying stints with Premiership side Newcastle Falcons and French juggernauts Rugby Club Toulonnais.

the sense was that this could be a watershed moment for the country. As it was, however, Rugby World Cup 2003 proved to be a low point for Tonga as they failed to win a game.

But from that disappointment came motivation, and Tonga returned in France four years later fired up. They boasted an impressive squad, including the likes of flanker Nili Latu and number eight Finau Maka, and claimed two wins at a tournament for the first time. It was only a narrow 30-25 loss to South Africa, eventual champions, that stopped Tonga making the quarter-finals.

Tonga should have made the quarter-finals four years later, as they pulled off a stunning 19-14 win over France in the pool stage. Frustratingly, they had lost to Canada before that and, as a result, France took second place by virtue of them having more bonus points.

Tonga very nearly pulled off another shock win against France at Rugby World Cup 2019. Les Bleus raced into a 17-point lead during their game in Japan and seemed to be cruising but Tonga reeled them in and only narrowly lost 23-21.

It was a typical performance from Tonga, full of heart and passion, and they just refused to give up even when the odds seemed against them.

"In Tonga it's like this: number one is our faith, family, rugby and then comes food," Tonga full-back Telusa Veainu said during Rugby World Cup 2019.

"That's what we play for: our country. We're just against the world really."

After years battling away at rugby's top table, Tonga will be hoping that France is the moment they break through and reach the knockout stages.

RUGBY WORLD CUP PERFORMANCES

1987 .... Pool stage
1991 .... Did not qualify
1995 .... Pool stage
1999 .... Pool stage
2003 .... Pool stage
2007 .... Pool stage
2011 .... Pool stage
2015 .... Pool stage
2019 .... Pool stage

POOL B

Romania

After missing out on Rugby World Cup 2019, Romania are back on rugby's biggest stage. Following head coach Andy Robinson's resignation in December 2022, Eugen Apjok is now in charge and wants to build on the foundations his predecessor laid. There is plenty of work to do, but Romania want to grow.

Above: Romania last played at a Rugby World Cup back in 2015.

Rugby World Cup 2019 was a painful experience for Romania as, for the first time in their history, they were not part of the tournament. Instead, they could only watch on as the other sides did battle on the biggest stage of all.

Before that, Romania had appeared at every Rugby World Cup and they have enjoyed some memorable moments along the way. They won their first Rugby World Cup match in their opening game of the inaugural tournament in 1987, beating Zimbabwe by a solitary point.

Romania followed that up by beating Fiji four years later and they have only failed to win a match at Rugby World Cup 1995 and 2011.

They have never made it past the pool stage but some of their wins live long in the memory, none more so than their one in 2015 when they mounted a thrilling comeback to beat Canada 17-15. Florin Vlaicu kicked the winning points in the dying moments, and the celebrations afterwards summed up what it meant to the players.

It was a big victory for Romania as at the tournament before that they had lost all four of their matches in New Zealand. That was a blow, particularly as at Rugby World Cup 2007 they had beaten Portugal and narrowly lost 24-18 to Italy. Romania did suffer an 85-8 defeat to New Zealand at that tournament, while four years earlier they lost 90-8 to Australia.

Losses like that, though, appear to be a thing of the past and Romania have become more defensively solid over the

RWC STATS

Played: 28
Won: 6
Lost: 22
Drawn: 0
Winning percentage: 21%
Points for: 365
Points against: 1,068
Biggest victory: 37-7
v Namibia in Launceston on 30 October, 2003
Heaviest defeat: 90-8
v Australia in Brisbane on 18 October, 2003
World Rugby Men's Rankings powered by Capgemini: 20

COACH

EUGEN APJOK

After Andy Robinson resigned in December 2022, Romania acted fast to appoint native Eugen Apjok as their new interim head coach. A fly-half during his playing days, Apjok knows the Romania setup having previously worked as a backs coach at Rugby World Cup 2015. He has excelled as a head coach domestically too with Romanian club CSM Știința Baia Mare. Apjok has worked with them since 2003 and led them to the league title in each of the past four years.

STAR PLAYER

MIHAI MACOVEI

Position: .... Flanker, number eight
Born: ....29 October, 1986, Gura Humorului, Romania
Club: .... Rugby Club bassin d'Arcachon (FRA)
Height: 1.95m (6ft 5in)
Weight: 108kg (17st)
Caps: 101
Points: .... 105 (21 tries)

Mihai Macovei has enjoyed a brilliant career and undoubtedly goes down as one of the greats of Romanian rugby. He achieved his 100th cap for his country in 2022; that is a remarkable feat, given he made his debut for them all the way back in 2006. A powerful forward, Macovei earned 68 of his 100 caps as captain of Romania and he regularly leads by example. That was certainly the case at Rugby World Cup 2015, when he scored two tries in the closing stages as Romania came back to beat Canada 17-15.

years. Indeed, in 2015 they ran Italy close again, this time losing 32-22.

After missing out on the last Rugby World Cup, Romania moved to appoint Andy Robinson in September 2019. The former England flanker boasts an impressive CV, which includes stints in charge of England and Scotland, but he had been out of work since 2016.

During his time in charge he set about revamping Romania's setup, particularly trying to raise the intensity in training to make the players fitter. Robinson drew inspiration from Japan in that regard, with many of their squad highlighting tough training as part of the reason they made the quarter-finals of Rugby World Cup 2019. A 24-17 defeat to Argentina in 2021 underlined how Romania are growing more competitive, but Robinson resigned after five wins in 11 matches in 2022.

His successor, Eugen Apjok, appreciates the work Robinson has done and is aiming to quickly build on the foundations ahead of the tournament in France. Apjok represented Romania during his playing days and has since gone on to become an impressive coach. He enjoyed great success domestically with Romanian club CSM Știința Baia Mare and now wants to succeeed on the international stage.

It will not be easy, especially given the strong teams in Romania's pool, but Apjok is relishing the challenge ahead of him. "My appointment as coach of the national team is an honour, and at the same time, a great challenge and responsibility," said Apjok. "We can build around a common vision to reflect as faithfully as possible the culture and spirit of Romanian rugby."

Romania have always vowed to punch above their weight and Rugby World Cup 2023 will be no different. They are not there to simply make up the numbers.

RUGBY WORLD CUP PERFORMANCES

1987 .... Pool stage
1991 .... Pool stage
1995 .... Pool stage
1999 .... Pool stage
2003 .... Pool stage
2007 .... Pool stage
2011 .... Pool stage
2015 .... Pool stage
2019 .... Did not qualify

France upstage All Blacks to make the final

31 October, 1999: Twickenham, London

Going into this Rugby World Cup semi-final, few people believed that France would have what it took to stop New Zealand. The All Blacks had looked in brilliant form and, after they raced into a 24-10 lead at Twickenham, the pre-match predictions looked spot on. France, however, fought back and pulled off one of the greatest comebacks in Rugby World Cup history. Christophe Lamaison proved to be the star of the show, after only being in the team at all following an injury to fellow fly-half Thomas Castaignède. Lamaison seized his moment, though, scoring a try and then putting in a flawless performance with the boot. He was at the heart of France's comeback, as they scored 33 unanswered points in 28 minutes to win 43-31.

Right: France were trailing 24-10 at one stage, but roared back to beat New Zealand.

Wales

With Warren Gatland at the helm, Wales became one of the most consistent performers at recent Rugby World Cups. After stepping down in 2019 and being replaced by Wayne Pivac, it looked like Wales fans had seen the last of Gatland but the New Zealander made a sensational return in December 2022.

Above: Wales made it to the semi-finals of Rugby World Cup 2011.

It is little wonder there was so much excitement in Wales when it was confirmed that Warren Gatland would be returning for a second spell in charge. During his first stint, 2007-19, Gatland transformed Wales into one of the best teams in the world. It was hoped that Wayne Pivac could build on Gatland's success when he was hired in the wake of Rugby World Cup 2019, but the results did not follow. Eventually, after a disappointing 2022, which saw Wales come fifth in the Six Nations and lose to Georgia, Pivac was dismissed.

Under Gatland, Wales reached two semi-finals and a quarter-final at three Rugby World Cups and, had things gone differently, they could have easily achieved more. That was certainly the case in 2011, when Wales were narrowly beaten 9-8 by France in the semi-finals. It was a tight, tense affair and Wales so nearly pulled off a major victory despite having their captain Sam Warburton sent off after 19 minutes. Stephen Jones hit the post with a conversion after Mike Phillips had darted over to score and then Leigh Halfpenny came up just short when he attempted to slot a late penalty. It was heartbreak for Wales and another narrow defeat to South Africa sent them home in the quarter-finals of Rugby World Cup 2015, but only after they had ensured England would be eliminated in the pool stage as hosts by beating them 28-25 at Twickenham.

Four years later in Japan, in what was meant to be Gatland's last Rugby

WRU

RWC STATS

Played: 44
Won: 26
Lost: 18
Drawn: 0
Winning percentage: 59.1%
Points for: 1,238
Points against: 865
Biggest victory: 81-7
v Namibia in Cardiff
on 26 September, 2011
Heaviest defeat: 49-6
v New Zealand in Brisbane
on 14 June, 1987
World Rugby Men's Rankings powered by Capgemini: 10

COACH

WARREN GATLAND

After leaving Wales in 2019, Warren Gatland returned to his native New Zealand to work with Super Rugby side, the Chiefs. He got the call to return to Wales in December 2022 and he will be aiming to emulate the success he had during his first spell. During that first stint in charge of Wales, Gatland led Wales to two Rugby World Cup semi-finals and four Six Nations titles, including three Grand Slams.

STAR PLAYER

DAN BIGGAR

Position: .... Fly-half
Born: .... 16 October, 1989, Morriston, Wales
Club: ....Rugby Club Toulonnais (FRA)
Height: 1.88m (6ft 2in)
Weight: 93kg (14st 7lb)
Caps: ....106 (+3 Lions)
Points: .... 599 (7 tries)

Dan Biggar has come a long way since making his debut for Wales as a 19-year-old. That was all the way back in 2008 and since then he has gone on to make over 100 appearances for his country. The fly-half has rightly earned a reputation as one of the fiercest competitors on the planet and it is no surprise to those who know him that he has progressed to captaining Wales at times. Ice cool under pressure, Biggar has become an expert at controlling games and his accuracy from the kicking tee makes him vital to Wales' chance of success.

World Cup with Wales, they once again made the semi-finals. After a nail-biting 20-19 win over France in the quarter-finals, spirits were high, but South Africa squeezed past them 19-16 on their way to eventually becoming world champions. That was the closest anyone came to beating the Springboks in the knockout stages, with England being blown away 32-12 in the final.

Rugby World Cup 2019 brought an end to Gatland's first stint with Wales and his success is even more impressive when compared to the country's previous records at tournaments. They reached the semi-final of the inaugural Rugby World Cup in 1987, losing to eventual winners New Zealand, but after that they experienced a period of boom and bust. They crashed out in the pool stage in 1991 and 1995, with the former including a shock defeat to Western Samoa. In 1999 and 2003 they made the quarter-finals, but that was followed up by another pool-stage exit at Rugby World Cup 2007. That tournament took place in France and Wales will be hoping they can make better memories this time around.

That was Pivac's aim when he was appointed by Wales in 2019, and there were undoubtedly some highs during his time in charge. In 2021, he led Wales to Six Nations glory, with only a narrow 32-30 defeat to France denying them the Grand Slam. Either side of that, though, Wales finished fifth in the 2020 and 2022 Six Nations, and the biggest challenge for Pivac was ensuring a level of consistency with performances. That was Gatland's greatest strength, as he turned one of the tournament's smaller nations into a rugby powerhouse. Do not bet against him doing it again.

RUGBY WORLD CUP PERFORMANCES

1987 .... Third
1991 .... Pool stage
1995 .... Pool stage
1999 .... Quarter-final
2003 .... Quarter-final
2007 .... Pool stage
2011 .... Fourth
2015 .... Quarter-final
2019 .... Fourth

Australia

After a period of impressive dominance at Rugby World Cups during the 1990s, Australia want to get their hands back on the famous Webb Ellis Cup. They suffered a disappointing quarter-final exit at the last tournament in Japan but are determined to bounce back with Eddie Jones back in charge.

Above: The 1990s was a golden period for Australia, as they won two Rugby World Cups.

In the formative years of Rugby World Cup, you would have struggled to find a more dominant team than Australia. The Wallabies reached the semi-finals of the inaugural tournament in 1987, which they hosted alongside New Zealand, but France and the dancing feet of full-back Serge Blanco defeated them 30-24.

Four years later, though, Australia travelled to the northern hemisphere and won their first Rugby World Cup. That was a side blessed with legends such as David Campese and John Eales, and no one could find a way to stop them.

After a disappointing Rugby World Cup in 1995, where as holders the Wallabies went out in the quarter-finals, they were once again crowned world champions in 1999. Eales was this time skippering the side and the emergence of the likes of fly-half Stephen Larkham gave fresh blood to a team packed with experience. They were a cut above sides at that tournament and their 35-12 victory over France in the final summed up their dominance.

After winning two of the first four Rugby World Cups, Australia are still waiting to get their hands on a third. Both of their two triumphs came in the northern hemisphere and it is partly why they will head to France this time around dreaming of upsetting the odds. The Wallabies also finished runners-up during another northern hemisphere Rugby World Cup – the 2015 edition that England hosted – and

Wallabies

RWC STATS

Played: 53
Won: 42
Lost: 11
Drawn: 0
Winning percentage: 79.2%
Points for: 1,797
Points against: 754
Biggest victory: 142-0
v Namibia in Adelaide
on 25 October, 2003
Heaviest defeat: 40-16
v England in Oita
on 19 October, 2019
World Rugby Men's Rankings powered by Capgemini: 7

COACH

EDDIE JONES

After being relieved of his duties by England in December 2022, Eddie Jones made a shock return to management only a month later by taking charge of Australia. This is Jones' second stint in charge of the Wallabies and back in 2003 he led them to the Rugby World Cup final, before they were beaten by England in Sydney. Jones will get two chances to avenge that painful loss after signing a contract until 2027.

STAR PLAYER

MICHAEL HOOPER

Position: .... Flanker
Born: .... 29 October, 1991, Sydney, Australia
Club: .... Waratahs (AUS)
Height: 1.82m (6ft)
Weight: 101kg (15st 8lb)
Caps: 124
Points: .... 110 (22 tries)

After making his debut for Australia in 2012, Michael Hooper has gone on to have a glittering career with the Wallabies. From a young age he was tipped for the top and he has more than lived up to the hype. Hooper is one of the best flankers on the planet, and his ability to turn the ball over makes him a menace at the breakdown. He is the Wallabies' most-capped captain and has also won the John Eales Medal, an award for the best Australian player each year, more times than anyone else. Still with years ahead of him, Hooper is already a legend.

that was a prime example of how they can come into a tournament being written off, but eventually defy the critics. Just a year out from that Rugby World Cup, Australia had been reeling after head coach Ewen McKenzie resigned, but in came Michael Cheika and he led them to the final, where they were eventually undone by a brilliant New Zealand team.

Cheika and Australia did not enjoy such a successful Rugby World Cup in 2019, crashing out in the quarter-finals to England. It was a disappointing performance from the Wallabies, who could not cope with England's pace and power, falling to a 40-16 defeat. After that, Australia and Cheika decided to part ways. Dave Rennie took the reins after the last Rugby World Cup, but he was replaced by former boss Eddie Jones in January 2023.

After winning Rugby World Cup 1999, Australia suffered from inconsistency at the tournament, and the hope is that Jones can change that during his second spell in charge.

The Wallabies reached the final in 2003, losing in the dying seconds of extra-time to England as Jonny Wilkinson kicked a drop goal, but four years later they exited at the quarter-final stage. Rugby World Cup 2011 saw them go one better, but they were eliminated in the semi-finals by eventual winners New Zealand.

Australia will be hoping to go deep into the tournament in France and rekindle their glory years. Jones' return caught many by surprise as only a month earlier he had been let go by England. The Australian is out to make the Wallabies a force again, particularly after he narrowly missed out on winning Rugby World Cup 2003 with them during his first stint in charge.

RUGBY WORLD CUP PERFORMANCES

1987 .... Fourth
1991 .... CHAMPIONS
1995 .... Quarter-final
1999 .... CHAMPIONS
2003 .... Runners-up
2007 .... Quarter-final
2011 .... Third
2015 .... Runners-up
2019 .... Quarter-final

FLYING FIJIANS

Fiji

Regarded as one of the most entertaining teams on the planet, Fiji are working to add substance to their style. The growth of the club game is helping their progress and Simon Raiwalui has now been charged with making them a force to be reckoned with in France. Whatever happens, though, Fiji are sure to get fans off their seats.

Above: Fiji players celebrate after reaching the quarter-finals of Rugby World Cup 2007.

Returning to France for Rugby World Cup 2023 will bring back fond memories for Fiji of arguably their finest-ever hour. The last time a tournament was held there, back in 2007, Fiji put in some brilliant performances to get all the way to the quarter-finals.

They had a side packed with attacking talent and flair, and after squeezing past Japan 35-31 in their opening game, Fiji set their sights on reaching the quarter-finals. They duly went into their final pool game against Wales knowing it was a winner-takes-all clash, with Australia already set to finish top. What followed was an enthralling match, as the Welsh opted to go toe-to-toe with Fiji and play a game full of attacking, running rugby.

It was a bold call from Wales but it looked like it would pay off for them as they were on course for victory before Graham Dewes scored the decisive try for Fiji with three minutes to go. That handed Fiji a 38-34 victory and the scenes at full-time summed up what it meant to the island nation.

Their only other previous quarter-final had come all the way back in 1987 at the inaugural Rugby World Cup in Australia and New Zealand. Fiji finished second in their pool to eventual winners New Zealand and they then came unstuck in the quarter-finals against a strong France side. The hope was Fiji could build on that showing; however, they struggled in the following

RWC STATS

Played: 32
Won: 11
Lost: 21
Drawn: 0
Winning percentage: 34.3%
Points for: 732
Points against: 974
Biggest victory: 67-18 v Namibia in Béziers on 1 October, 1999
Heaviest defeat: 66-0 v Wales in Hamilton on 2 October, 2011
World Rugby Men's Rankings powered by Capgemini: 14

COACH

SIMON RAIWALUI

After Vern Cotter stepped down as head coach in February 2023, Fiji moved to appoint Simon Raiwalui. Previously the General Manager High Performance of Fiji, Raiwalui was chosen because he knows the current set-up well. Before that, he had spent time coaching in Australia and France. Raiwalui enjoyed an impressive playing career, representing clubs such as Saracens and Racing 92. He also played for, and captained, Fiji.

STAR PLAYER

LEVANI BOTIA

Position: .... Centre
Born: .... 14 March, 1989, Naivucini, Fiji
Club: .... Stade Rochelais (FRA)
Height: 1.80m (5ft 11in)
Weight: 105kg (16st 7lb)
Caps: 22
Points: .... 25 (5 tries)

The fact that Levani Botia's nickname is "Demolition Man" should tell you all you need to know about how powerful an opponent he is. Blessed with pace and power, Botia is a nightmare for defenders to deal with. He actually began life working as a prison warden before being picked to play for Fiji's rugby sevens team. That eventually landed him a move to French club Stade Rochelais and he has been thriving in Europe ever since. Capable of playing in the centres or as a forward, Botia is a rare breed of player who can excel in multiple positions if needed.

tournaments. In 1991 they failed to get out of their pool and in 1995 they did not even qualify for the tournament.

A quarter-final play-off four years later gave reason for optimism but, other than 2007, Fiji have not managed to get out out of their pool. The country has long produced some of the finest athletes in rugby, with many of them moving to France to ply their club trade. The challenge has always been bringing them together and making them gel on the international stage, but Simon Raiwalui is confident he can succeed, despite only taking charge in February 2023.

Rugby sevens is still proving a useful production line for talent, with many of the current squad having made their first steps in the game there before moving to 15s. Fiji won the gold medal in rugby sevens at the Rio Olympics in 2016, which gave the country a big lift, but the club game in the region has also recently received a major boost, too.

From 2022, the Pacific region was introduced to Super Rugby, which has historically played host to club sides from Australia, New Zealand and South Africa. Two teams were added – Fijian Drua and Moana Pasifika – to make it a 12-team competition under the new name of Super Rugby Pacific. It is a huge step forward for Fiji and the other Pacific Island nations, as players now have a club side closer to home. "The South Pacific has traditionally been the game's talent gold mine globally, but NZR [New Zealand Rugby] and RA's [Rugby Australia's] commitment will help us provide professional pathways for our players right here at home," said Fiji Rugby CEO John O'Connor.

Whatever happens in France, the future looks bright for Fiji.

RUGBY WORLD CUP PERFORMANCES

1987 .... Quarter-final
1991 .... Pool stage
1995 .... Did not qualify
1999 .... Quarter-final play-off
2003 .... Pool stage
2007 .... Quarter-final
2011 .... Pool stage
2015 .... Pool stage
2019 .... Pool stage

Georgia

Georgia continue to improve every year, as they test themselves against more top opponents. In 2022, they claimed famous victories against Italy and Wales. Now the aim and challenge is to make their mark at a Rugby World Cup by reaching the quarter-finals for the first time. It's a tall order, but you would be foolish to rule it out.

Above: Georgia are bidding to make their first-ever Rugby World Cup quarter-final.

Rugby World Cup 2023 will mark 20 years since Georgia made their tournament debut, and they have come an incredibly long way in that time.

During that first tournament in 2003, Georgia failed to win a single game and endured the pain of suffering an opening 84-6 defeat by England.

Those days are now very much in the past and Georgia are beginning to establish themselves as one of the fastest-growing rugby nations.

They have made progress since their Rugby World Cup debut, but 2022 really was a landmark year for Georgia. In July, they beat Italy 28-19 to claim their first-ever win over a Six Nations side.

Just four months later, they had another – and this time it was an even bigger scalp, with Georgia beating Wales 13-12 in Cardiff. Luka Matkava was the hero on the day, kicking a 78th-minute penalty to spark wild celebrations among the Georgia players.

"Before the game, I said [to the team] if you believe, you can win. The boys said yes," Georgia head coach Levan Maisashvili said.

"At half-time, I said you can win this game. That result was very important for us, for self-belief, for trust in our system, for trusting each other, coaches and players."

The result was even more special for Georgia as it came just a year after Maisashvili had battled with Covid-19.

"I was 60kg, I lost 25kg and I couldn't move my hands, my head, just only watching, only my brain surviving," Maisashvili told World Rugby.

RWC STATS

Played: 20
Won: 5
Lost: 15
Drawn: 0
Winning percentage: 25%
Points for: 262
Points against: 646
Biggest victory: 30-0 v Namibia in Lens on 26 September, 2007
Heaviest defeat: 84-6 v England in Perth on 12 October, 2003
World Rugby Men's Rankings powered by Capgemini: 12

COACH

LEVAN MAISASHVILI

Since taking charge of Georgia in 2020, Levan Maisashvili has pulled off some brilliant results. He guided Georgia to wins over Italy and Wales in 2022, while Georgia also won the Rugby Europe Championship to qualify for Rugby World Cup 2023. Maisashvili has also battled back from severe Covid-19 in 2021, when he was given a one per cent chance of survival by doctors as he lost 25kg, and could not move his head or hands.

STAR PLAYER

DAVIT NINIASHVILI

Position: .... Wing, full-back
Born: .... 14 July, 2002, Tbilisi, Georgia
Club: .... Lyon Olympique Universitaire (FRA)
Height: 1.86m (6ft 1in)
Weight: 85kg (13st 5lb)
Caps: 19
Points: .... 38 (7 tries)

Georgia have long been known for producing some of the best props in the world, but Davit Niniashvili is evidence of how they are broadening their horizons. He may be young but the winger is already making waves for both club and country. Niniashvili was exceptional as Georgia beat Italy in July 2022, and he has become a regular for Lyon Olympique Universitaire, too. Niniashvili signed for them in 2021 as a hot prospect, but by the end of that season he was starring in the Challenge Cup, setting a new record for the most defenders beaten in the final as Lyon defeated Rugby Club Toulonnais.

The head coach contracted Covid-19 while Georgia were playing in South Africa in July 2021, which was a great chance for them to test themselves against a top side.

The Covid-19 pandemic disrupted the tour, forcing the second test to be cancelled, and it also left Maisashvili fighting for his life.

"For approximately 28 days I was in a coma," he said. "They gave me a one or two per cent [chance] for life."

Maisashvili has recovered and, after leading Georgia to a stellar 2022, he is taking them to Rugby World Cup 2023. His story is an inspiring one, and so is Georgia's rugby journey.

After failing to win a game at the 2003 tournament, four years later they claimed a first victory by beating Namibia. They also pushed Ireland all the way, narrowly losing 14-10.

That was a glimpse of the future and, after claiming one win at Rugby World Cup 2011, Georgia caught the eye in 2015. For the first time, they claimed two wins and finished third in their pool, making them automatic qualifiers for Rugby World Cup 2019.

They failed to replicate that feat at the last tournament in Japan, which means they had to qualify for France this time. Georgia impressed during that process, though, and their style of play has developed under Maisashvili.

Usually known for strong forward play, Georgia have added flair to their game and their backline has been causing teams problems. Exciting wing Davit Niniashvili sums up their new impetus and he already looks at home on the big stage after shining in French club rugby.

The future looks bright for Georgia, and France could be the moment they truly establish themselves.

In the space of 20 years they have achieved so much – and the best is yet to come.

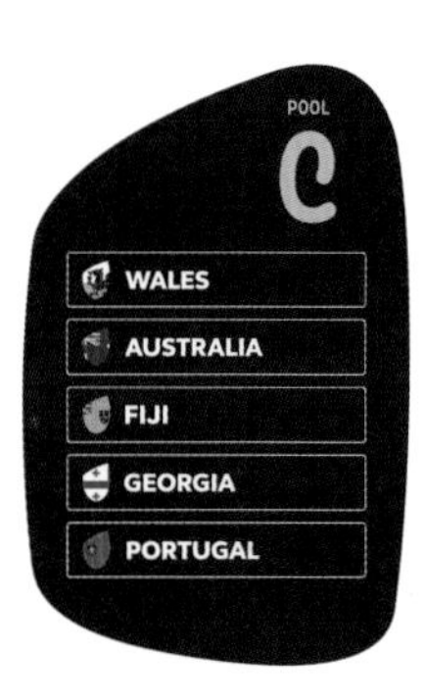

RUGBY WORLD CUP PERFORMANCES

1987 .... Did not enter
1991 .... Did not enter
1995 .... Did not qualify
1999 .... Did not qualify
2003 .... Pool stage
2007 .... Pool stage
2011 .... Pool stage
2015 .... Pool stage
2019 .... Pool stage

Portugal

Portugal qualified for Rugby World Cup 2023 in dramatic fashion by winning the Final Qualification Tournament. France will be only their second Rugby World Cup and they travel there hoping to secure their first-ever win at a tournament. It will not be easy but, under head coach Patrice Lagisquet, Portugal continue to improve.

Above: Portugal's last Rugby World Cup appearance came back in 2007.

Portugal are back at a Rugby World Cup for the first time since 2007 and they will be determined to give a good account of themselves in France.

Head coach Patrice Lagisquet believes there are around four million Portuguese people living in France and that they can only help his team.

"We know that they will have a lot of support," he said. "The idea will be to be competitive and above all not to be pushovers, which was slightly the case in 2007 in certain matches."

Rugby World Cup 2007, which also took place in France, was Portugal's debut appearance, and it was a steep learning curve for them.

They were drawn in a tough pool, which included Italy, New Zealand and Scotland, and they got off to a difficult start by losing 56-10 to the Scots. That was then followed up by a 108-13 loss to the All Blacks, who ran riot in Lyon.

After those opening two games, Portugal began to settle, though, and they went down 31-5 to Italy. Their best performance came against Romania, however, and they took the lead against them before narrowly losing 14-10.

The whole tournament was an incredible experience for Portugal, who received plenty of support. The players were full of emotion as well and at each match the national anthem was belted out by them, with a few of the squad close to tears.

"We had to exceed in very adverse conditions, we had to train a lot, it was a completely amateur team but had a professional spirit," Portugal's head

PORTUGAL RUGBY

RWC STATS

Played: 4
Won: 0
Lost: 4
Drawn: 0
Winning percentage: 0%
Points for: 38
Points against: 209
Biggest victory: N/A
Heaviest defeat: 108-13 v New Zealand in Lyon on 15 September, 2007
World Rugby Men's Rankings powered by Capgemini: 16

COACH

PATRICE LAGISQUET

After enjoying a glittering playing career on the wing for France, in which he earned the nickname "The Bayonne Express", Patrice Lagisquet is hoping to make his mark at a Rugby World Cup as a coach. He boasts an impressive CV after being head coach at Biarritz and working as an assistant for the French national team. Lagisquet has shone since being hired by Portugal in 2019, helping them qualify for only their second-ever Rugby World Cup.

STAR PLAYER

SAMUEL MARQUES

Position: .... Scrum-half
Born: .... 8 December, 1988, Condom, France
Club: .... US Carcassonne (FRA)
Height: 1.74m (5ft 7in)
Weight: 76kg (11st 13lb)
Caps: 19
Points: .... 185 (2 tries)

Born in France, Samuel Marques wrote himself into Portuguese rugby history by playing a pivotal role in helping them qualify for Rugby World Cup 2023. The scrum-half secured a draw against USA with the last kick of the game, which meant Portugal won the Final Qualification Tournament and booked a place in France. Marques' kicking makes him a valuable asset for Portugal. He had been out of the team for seven years, until he was recalled in 2020 by new head coach Patrice Lagisquet. Marques has shone since then, using his wealth of experience from years of playing club rugby in France.

coach from 2007, Tomaz Morais, told World Rugby.

"Many times we would train in the very early hours of the day at 6.30am and then we would train again in the evening."

Portugal have come a long way since 2007 and have recorded some impressive results, most notably a 25-25 draw with Georgia in 2022. Head coach Lagisquet views Georgia as the blueprint for Portugal to follow.

When he took charge the squad was packed with young players, but he has bolstered it by recalling the likes of scrum-half Samuel Marques – who was playing in France.

"It was not easy on a daily basis, there were still some disappointments," said Lagisquet. "We had to attract interest from professional players in France in order to enable amateur players from Portugal to become pros. We had to combine a lot of factors to achieve this result."

As Lagisquet points out, Portugal's road to Rugby World Cup 2023 was not an easy one. They finished third in the Rugby Europe Championship, meaning they joined the Final Qualification Tournament.

Portugal kicked that off with wins against Hong Kong (42-14) and Kenya (85-0), meaning it was a straight shootout between them and USA in the final match.

Portugal knew that a draw would be good enough for them given their superior points difference and they got that in dramatic fashion.

Marques slotted a kick with literally the last play of the game to secure a 16-16 draw and book Portugal's place in France.

"There was also a huge desire from most of these players," said Lagisquet. "That's what was pretty awesome to experience, everything they gave to go after this dream that became a reality."

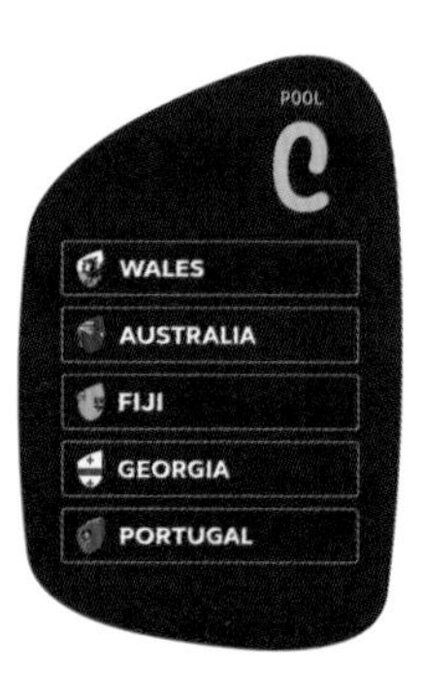

RUGBY WORLD CUP PERFORMANCES

1987 .... Did not play
1991 .... Did not qualify
1995 .... Did not qualify
1999 .... Did not qualify
2003 .... Did not qualify
2007 .... Pool stage
2011 .... Did not qualify
2015 .... Did not qualify
2019 .... Did not qualify

Corleto and Argentina silence Paris

7 September, 2007: Stade de France, Saint-Denis

As hosts of Rugby World Cup 2007, the pressure was on France to deliver. No more so was that evident than in the opening game of the tournament when they took on Argentina. The South American side were written off going into the game, with many expecting them to fall to defeat in front of a vocal Stade de France crowd. What followed, however, was a brilliant performance from Argentina that was full of heart and fight. They produced moments of real quality too, no more so than when Ignacio Corleto scored in the first half. Argentina intercepted the ball and eventually Corleto found himself in space, and he left the French defenders in his wake as he scored in the corner. Suddenly, the Stade de France was silenced.

Right: Ignacio Corleto's try against France was the start of a magical Rugby World Cup for Argentina.

RUGBY
2007
adidas
UAR
15

England

After suffering heartbreak in the final of Rugby World Cup 2019, England are determined to go all the way in France. They have endured a period of transition since the last tournament four years ago, but have the quality in their squad to beat any side on their day and will fear no one.

Above: England's one and only Rugby World Cup triumph came in 2003

Rugby World Cup 2019 was a case of so near, yet so far for England. After a dazzling victory over New Zealand in the semi-finals, Eddie Jones' side had looked on course to go all the way at the tournament for the first time since 2003. In the end, however, they came up short in the final as South Africa defeated them to leave England heading home heartbroken.

Other than 2003, that is very much the story of England's Rugby World Cup history, and they have now finished runners-up on three occasions. The first of those came in 1991 as Australia beat them in the final, but the second loss was in 2007 as once again South Africa proved to be their downfall. That defeat to the Springboks took place in France, and England will hope they can return to Paris this time around and banish those memories.

Prior to winning Rugby World Cup 2003, England had a chequered history in the tournament, as in 1995 they made the semi-finals, and in 1987 and 1999 they crashed out in the quarter-finals. The second of those quarter-final losses came under head coach Clive Woodward and, over the following four years, he transformed England into the number one team in the world ahead of the tournament in Australia.

Under Woodward, England developed a formidable forward pack that included the likes of captain Martin Johnson and Lawrence Dallaglio. The backs were just as dangerous too, with wing Jason Robinson's move from rugby league

RWC STATS

Played: 50
Won: 36
Lost: 14
Drawn: 0
Winning percentage: 72%
Points for: 1,569
Points against: 783
Biggest victory: .... 111-13 v Uruguay in Brisbane on 2 November, 2003
Heaviest defeat: .... 36-0 v South Africa in Saint-Denis on 14 September, 2007
World Rugby Men's Rankings powered by Capgemini: 6

COACH

STEVE BORTHWICK

Hired by the RFU in December 2022, Steve Borthwick was put in charge of England after they parted ways with Eddie Jones. Borthwick enjoyed an impressive playing career, captaining England, and has made a strong start to his time as a coach. He worked as a forwards coach for Japan and then England, both times under Jones, before taking charge of Leicester Tigers. Borthwick did well there, guiding the Tigers to the Premiership title in 2022.

STAR PLAYER

MARO ITOJE

Position: .... Second-row
Born: ....28 October, 1994, London, England
Club: .... Saracens (ENG)
Height: 1.95m (6ft 5in)
Weight: 115kg (18st 2lb)
Caps: .... 65 (+6 Lions)
Points: .... 20 (4 tries)

Since making his England debut all the way back in 2016, Maro Itoje has gone on to establish himself as one of the best players on the planet. He usually operates in the second-row, but can play as a flanker, too – which underlines his incredible athleticism. Itoje has become a key part of England's team since breaking into the side, with his work in the lineout vital to their success. Although not England captain, Itoje has emerged as a leader in the squad and his ability to deliver in crunch moments makes him an example for others to follow.

to union providing the team with explosive pace out wide.

England headed to Australia in 2003 as one of the favourites and they lived up to their billing, eventually setting up a showdown with the Wallabies in the final. It proved to be a tense, tight game, with the boots of Elton Flatley and Jonny Wilkinson keeping the scoreboard ticking over for both teams. In the end, it was Wilkinson who became the hero, as he kicked the winning drop goal in the dying seconds to secure the Webb Ellis Cup for England with a 20-17 win in extra-time. That remains the greatest moment in English rugby history and the challenge for today's players is to become heroes themselves.

It looked like that would be the case in Japan in 2019, where England seemed unrecognisable from the team that crashed out in the pool stage four years earlier. Young stars such as Sam Underhill and Tom Curry rose to the occasion, as Jones' side topped their pool to qualify for the quarter-finals. It was there that England cruised past Australia and, after defeating holders New Zealand 19-7 in the semi-finals, the country's wait to be world champions again looked over. South Africa, however, showed their experience to defeat England in the final, and they were left licking their wounds.

England's development since then has been turbulent. They won the 2020 Six Nations, which was interrupted by the Covid-19 pandemic, but then finished fifth the following year and third 12 months after that. Mixed results led to head coach Eddie Jones losing his job and former England captain Steve Borthwick being handed the reins. Borthwick impressed as head coach of Leicester Tigers and he has a growing reputation within the game.

RUGBY WORLD CUP PERFORMANCES

1987 ....Quarter-final
1991 ....Runners-up
1995 ....Fourth
1999 ....Quarter-final
2003 ....CHAMPIONS
2007 ....Runners-up
2011 ....Quarter-final
2015 ....Pool stage
2019 ....Runners-up

POOL D

Japan

After impressing as hosts of Rugby World Cup 2019, Japan will be out to continue their rise at this tournament in France. Their development over the past few years has accelerated dramatically and they have earned a reputation as one of the most entertaining teams on the planet. Now they are out to shock the world again.

Above: Japan made history by making their first Rugby World Cup quarter-final in 2019.

All eyes were on Japan as hosts of the last Rugby World Cup and they rose to the occasion in style. As was the case in 2015, Japan set the ambitious target of getting out of their pool and reaching the quarter-finals. That was something they had never before achieved in their previous eight Rugby World Cup appearances, but on home soil they emphatically smashed through the glass ceiling.

Not only did Japan get out of Pool A but they topped it too, securing impressive victories against Ireland and Scotland. They had gone into the pool with many thinking they could sneak through in second place, but they laid down a marker by beating Ireland 19-12 in their second game. Not content with that, they then defeated Scotland 28-21, scoring three tries during a blistering attacking display in the first half.

The nation got swept along in the team's story and in the end it took South Africa, who would eventually go on to become world champions, to stop them in the quarter-finals. The Springboks were 26-3 winners in a game that felt like Japan had run out of steam after a huge effort during the pool stage. "Rugby is all about creating moments and taking opportunities," said Japan captain Michael Leitch after. "We had a few opportunities to capitalise on but unfortunately South Africa kicked us out. I'm extremely proud of what this team have done. To represent Asia

RWC STATS

Played: 33
Won: 8
Lost: 23
Drawn: 2
Winning percentage: 24.2%
Points for: 644
Points against: 1,347
Biggest victory: 52-8 v Zimbabwe in Belfast on 14 October, 1991
Heaviest defeat: 145-17 v New Zealand in Bloemfontein on 4 June, 1995
World Rugby Men's Rankings powered by Capgemini: 9

COACH

JAMIE JOSEPH

Since taking charge of Japan in 2016, Jamie Joseph has continued to grow his reputation as one of rugby's most talented coaches. He was under big pressure ahead of Rugby World Cup 2019, with Japan the hosts, but he managed to guide the country to their first-ever quarter-final appearance. Joseph has transformed Japan into an attacking side and he has been able to blood young players into the squad as well over the past few years.

STAR PLAYER

MICHAEL LEITCH

Position: .... Flanker
Born: ....23 October, 1988, Christchurch, New Zealand
Club: ... Toshiba Brave Lupus Tokyo (JPN)
Height: 1.89m (6ft 2in)
Weight: 113kg (17st 11lb)
Caps: 78
Points: ....100 (20 tries)

Michael Leitch has played a pivotal role in the rise of rugby in Japan and he is their true leader. Born in New Zealand, he moved to Japan as a teenager and has become an inspirational character on and off the pitch. Leitch leads by example and will have a big role to play in France. The flanker is renowned for delivering on big stages too, starring in the 2015 win over South Africa and throughout Rugby World Cup 2019. A tenacious defender, Leitch can be dangerous in attack as well, due to his strong running and ability to offload in the tackle.

and the tier two countries, I'm sure they'll be proud of us as well. Japan is only going to get stronger."

For around a decade Japan has been steadily improving as a rugby nation, and from 2013-14 they enjoyed a run of 10 straight wins under then head coach Eddie Jones. Jones was also in charge for Rugby World Cup 2015, where Japan really made their mark on the big stage by stunning South Africa in their opening game of the tournament. It remains one of, if not the biggest, shocks in rugby history, as winger Karne Hesketh scored a last-minute try to secure a 34-32 victory.

The famous win was even given the Hollywood treatment and turned into a movie, *The Brighton Miracle*. The popularity of rugby in Japan boomed after that victory, even if the Brave Blossoms went out in the pool stage.

Before that, Rugby World Cups had been painful affairs and stories of defeat, but now they are looked upon as moments to shine.

Since the last tournament, Japan's progress has been hampered by the Covid-19 pandemic – which stopped them playing any games in 2020. They have had some promising performances since then, though, running Ireland close in 2021 and pushing France all the way the following year.

That has all come with Jamie Joseph trying to blood new players into the squad at the same time as he casts an eye to the future. Young fly-half Seungsin Lee has caught the eye on occasion, as has scrum-half Naoto Saito. "We're a new team and we're really excited for the potential of this team," Joseph said. Now the question is, can Japan's new stars become history-makers too?

RUGBY WORLD CUP PERFORMANCES

1987 .... Pool stage
1991 .... Pool stage
1995 .... Pool stage
1999 .... Pool stage
2003 .... Pool stage
2007 .... Pool stage
2011 .... Pool stage
2015 .... Pool stage
2019 .... Quarter-final

Argentina

Argentina truly announced their arrival on the big stage by stunning everyone to make the semi-finals of Rugby World Cup 2007. Since then, they have gone from strength to strength and have the ability to beat anyone on their day. Los Pumas will want to bounce back after a disappointing performance at the last Rugby World Cup.

Above: Argentina announced their arrival on the big stage at Rugby World Cup 2007.

It is a sign of how much Argentina have grown as a rugby nation that a pool-stage exit at Rugby World Cup 2019 felt like a major disappointment. Argentina were admittedly drawn alongside England and France in the "Pool of Death", but given their past successes at tournaments they would have had aspirations of making the quarter-finals.

There was a time, however, when failing to get out of the pool stage was the norm for Los Pumas. That was the case for Argentina at the first three Rugby World Cups, as they found their feet on the international stage. They won just one game at those first three tournaments and it was clear that it would take time for the game to grow in the country.

A quarter-final appearance in 1999 was a sign of progress and things to come, with another pool-stage exit in 2003 only a blip as they truly announced their arrival four years later. That Rugby World Cup in 2007 was coincidentally in France, and Argentina will return to the country with brilliant memories from the last tournament there. They made their mark right from the off then, stunning hosts France in the opening game to claim a 17-12 win in Paris. "Argentina should be proud. I think we do exist," said Pumas captain Agustín Pichot after that victory. "We're not the best tactical players or the best technically, but our best resources are the passion and pride when we put on the jersey."

UAR

RWC STATS

Played: 41
Won: 21
Lost: 20
Drawn: 0
Winning percentage: 51.2%
Points for: 1,098
Points against: 839
Biggest victory: 67-14 v Namibia in Gosford on 14 October, 2003
Heaviest defeat: 46-15 v New Zealand in Wellington on 1 June, 1987
World Rugby Men's Rankings powered by Capgemini: 8

COACH

MICHAEL CHEIKA

Originally coming onboard as an adviser in 2020, Michael Cheika was made head coach of Argentina in March 2022 after Mario Ledesma stepped down. Cheika boasts a wealth of experience, guiding Australia to the Rugby World Cup final in 2015 just a year after taking over there. He made a similarly fast start to life with Argentina, masterminding them to a series win over Scotland during his first few months in charge of Los Pumas.

STAR PLAYER

JULIÁN MONTOYA

Position: ....Hooker
Born: ....29 October, 1993, Buenos Aires, Argentina
Club: .... Leicester Tigers (ENG)
Height: 1.83m (6ft)
Weight: 113kg (17st 11lb)
Caps: 85
Points: ....50 (10 tries)

Appointed as Argentina captain in 2021, Julián Montoya has risen to the challenge of being his country's skipper and leader. The hooker is a dynamic forward, capable of strong runs in the loose and crunching tackles as well. Despite playing in the front row, Montoya often has one of the highest tackle counts in games and his willingness to put his body on the line makes him an inspirational captain. In 2020, he moved to play his club rugby over in England after deciding to join Leicester Tigers. Montoya has impressed there, helping Leicester win the Premiership in 2022.

In 2007, Los Pumas went on to top Pool D and make the quarter-finals. Led by the brilliant half-back pairing of Pichot and Juan Martín Hernández, Argentina showed they were a force to be reckoned with and they navigated their way past Scotland to reach the semi-finals. It was there that they finally game unstuck, as South Africa, who went on to win the whole tournament, proved too much for them. However, rugby in Argentina had changed forever and it was no surprise that four years later they made the quarter-finals.

Following that tournament, Los Pumas joined the Rugby Championship in 2012 and they have benefited greatly from playing against Australia, New Zealand and South Africa every year. That much was clear at Rugby World Cup 2015, when they once again reached the semi-final, and this time they did it in style as they blew away Ireland 43-20 in the quarter-final.

It is performances like that which made Argentina's exit in the pool stage at Rugby World Cup 2019 so disappointing, although they only narrowly went down 23-21 to France – who pipped them to second place.

Never one to accept defeat, Argentina have fought back since then and, particularly under head coach Michael Cheika, they look a force again. Just months after taking charge in 2022, the Australian led Los Pumas to a series win over Scotland. Shortly after, Argentina claimed their biggest victory over Australia, winning 48-17, and that was followed up by a first-ever win against the All Blacks in New Zealand. Those wins reminded everyone of Argentina's quality and now the country will be dreaming of making more memories in France, just like they did at Rugby World Cup 2007.

RUGBY WORLD CUP PERFORMANCES

1987 .... Pool stage
1991 .... Pool stage
1995 .... Pool stage
1999 .... Quarter-final
2003 .... Pool stage
2007 .... Third
2011 .... Quarter-final
2015 .... Fourth
2019 .... Pool stage

Samoa

Western Samoa shocked everyone when they reached the quarter-finals of Rugby World Cup 1991 on their debut. Four years later they repeated that feat, but more recently Samoa have struggled to repeat those highs. They will be hoping that France can be a turning point and the start of an upturn in form at Rugby World Cups.

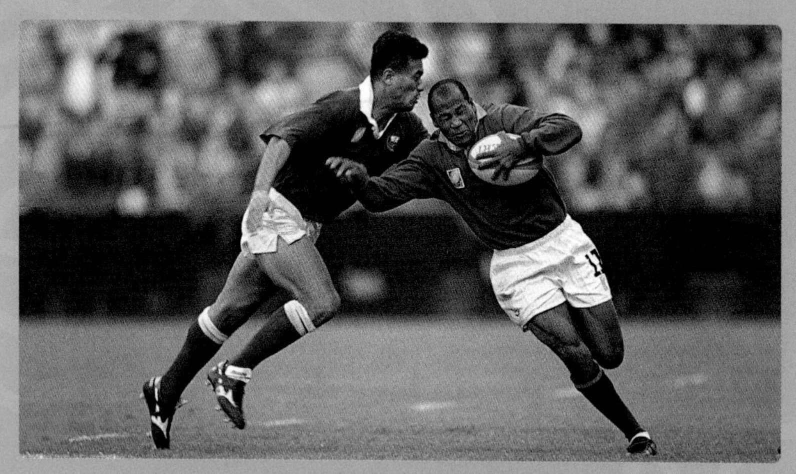

Above: Western Samoa reached the quarter-finals of Rugby World Cup 1995.

When Western Samoa arrived at Rugby World Cup 1991, little was expected of them. They were a country that had a playing population of just 2,000 and, as a result, the belief was that they would be on one of the first planes home.

That was not the feeling among the team, though, who boasted the likes of Apollo Perelini, Frank Bunce and Pat Lam. Also in their ranks was Brian Lima, whose nickname was "The Chiropractor" due to him being one of the toughest tacklers around. He went on to become the first player to compete at five Rugby World Cups, with 1991 his first.

"It's definitely the hardest tackle I've taken in my life but I'm still breathing and that's a good sign," South Africa fly-half Derick Hougaard said at Rugby World Cup 2003, after facing Lima.

Western Samoa laid down a marker on their Rugby World Cup debut in 1991, beating Wales 16-13 in front of a crowd of 45,000 at Cardiff Arms Park. It was a huge result and one that sent shockwaves around the rugby world.

The celebrations were wild and the significance of the result could not be summed up more than by the fact that try scorer To'o Vaega went on to name his son Cardiff in honour of the win.

The victory was followed up by a narrow 9-3 loss to Australia, who would go on to be champions, but Western Samoa recovered to defeat Argentina 35-12.

That set up a quarter-final with Scotland and they ultimately proved too strong for Western Samoa, who lost 28-6 at Murrayfield.

MANU SAMOA

RWC STATS

Played: 32
Won: 13
Lost: 19
Drawn: 0
Winning percentage: 39%
Points for: 712
Points against: 860
Biggest victory: 60-13 v Uruguay in Perth on 15 October, 2003
Heaviest defeat: 60-10 v South Africa in Brisbane on 1 November, 2003
World Rugby Men's Rankings powered by Capgemini: 11

COACH

SEILALA MAPUSUA

Put in charge of Samoa in August 2020, Seilala Mapusua has made a steady start to his first-ever head coach role. Mapusua enjoyed an impressive playing career before moving into coaching, making more than 100 appearances for English Premiership side London Irish and earning 26 caps for Samoa. He guided Samoa to Rugby World Cup qualification by beating Tonga over two legs. Mapusua has set his sights on blooding more local players into the Samoa team.

STAR PLAYER

MICHAEL ALAALATOA

Position: .... Prop
Born: ....28 August, 1991, Camperdown, Australia
Club: .... Leinster (IRE)
Height: 1.91m (6ft 3in)
Weight: 126kg (19st 9lb)
Caps: 12
Points: 0

Rugby very much runs in the family for Michael Alaalatoa as his dad, Vili, also represented Samoa. In fact, he was part of the famous Western Samoa side who stunned Wales at Rugby World Cup 1991. Now Alaalatoa is hoping to follow in his father's footsteps and make waves in France with Samoa. He has established himself as one of the finest props in the world. Alaalatoa currently plays for Irish side Leinster, but before that he was a regular for Super Rugby team the Crusaders. Born in Sydney, Alaalatoa's brother, Allan, is also a rugby player and he represents Australia.

They had announced themselves to the world, though, and put themselves on the rugby map. Going into Rugby World Cup 1995, they were no longer an unknown quantity – but still teams struggled to stop them.

Once again Western Samoa made the quarter-finals, beating Italy and Argentina but losing to England to finish second in Pool B. Waiting for them in the knockouts were hosts South Africa, who were the eventual winners of the tournament, and they defeated Western Samoa 42-14.

By Rugby World Cup 1999, Western Samoa had become Samoa, and they enjoyed another good tournament. Once again they claimed a famous win over Wales in Cardiff, beating them 38-31. That saw Samoa qualify for the quarter-final play-offs, but they failed to find a way past Scotland as they tried to reach a third quarter-final in a row.

Samoa have not returned to the knockout stages of a Rugby World Cup since then, but they have put in good performances over the years.

At Rugby World Cup 2003 they won two games, coming third in their pool behind England and South Africa. The same happened four years later, while at Rugby World Cup 2011 they also won two games – finishing third in Pool D behind South Africa and Wales.

The last two tournaments have been more disappointing for Samoa, though, as on both occasions they won just one game. That has forced them to have to qualify for the more recent Rugby World Cups, but they did so well for this tournament in France.

Samoa recorded a 79-28 aggregate win in a two-legged play-off against Tonga to reach France. The team has grown under new head coach Seilala Mapusua and there is belief they can compete well at Rugby World Cup 2023.

RUGBY WORLD CUP PERFORMANCES

1987 .... Did not play
1991 .... Quarter-final
1995 .... Quarter-final
1999 .... Quarter-final play-off
2003 .... Pool stage
2007 .... Pool stage
2011 .... Pool stage
2015 .... Pool stage
2019 .... Pool stage

POOL D

Chile

Chile will be making their Rugby World Cup debut in France after putting in some stunning qualifying performances. Head coach Pablo Lemoine has done a brilliant job since being appointed in 2018, improving the infrastructure of rugby in the country. Now, Chile have the chance to test themselves on the biggest stage of all.

Above: Chile are competing at their first-ever Rugby World Cup.

The rise of Chile has been remarkable and rapid. They had never qualified for a Rugby World Cup until this tournament, but head coach Pablo Lemoine has transformed the team and made their dreams come true.

Since his appointment as head coach in 2018, Chile have come a long way under Lemoine. In 2019, they lost 71-8 to the USA during a painful defeat. Three years later, they were beating the USA to qualify for Rugby World Cup 2023.

That victory came in July 2022 during an enthralling two-legged play-off. Chile looked as though they were heading for disappointment after losing the first leg at home 22-21.

It meant they needed to go to the USA and win. With just over 20 minutes to go, Chile were trailing by nine points on aggregate. Their Rugby World Cup dream looked like it was over.

But this team has developed a never-say-die attitude under Lemoine and they fought back, with Santiago Videla's late penalty securing a 31-29 victory and a 52-51 aggregate win. That brought an end to a tough qualification road for Chile, which began with them facing Brazil and Uruguay in a round-robin competition. Victory over Brazil but defeat to Uruguay led to them having to face Canada in a two-legged play-off.

Just as in the USA play-off, Chile lost the first leg 22-21 to Canada, but once again they bounced back to win the second 34-15. Videla was the hero once more too, scoring 23 points. That set up a play-off with the USA, which will go down in history for those in Chile.

RWC STATS

Played: 0
Won: 0
Lost: 0
Drawn: 0
Winning percentage: 0%
Points for: 0
Points against: 0
Biggest victory: N/A
Heaviest defeat: N/A
World Rugby Men's Rankings powered by Capgemini: 22

COACH

PABLO LEMOINE

After impressively guiding Uruguay to Rugby World Cup 2015, when they had failed to qualify for the previous two tournaments, Pablo Lemoine has worked wonders with Chile as well. He took charge of them in 2018 and has gradually improved them to secure qualification for their first-ever Rugby World Cup. Before becoming a coach, Lemoine played as a prop for Uruguay and featured in their first-ever Rugby World Cup match back in 1999.

STAR PLAYER

RODRIGO FERNÁNDEZ

Position: .... Fly-half, full-back
Born: ..... 8 February, 1996, Santiago, Chile
Club: .... Selknam (CHI)
Height: 1.83m (6ftin)
Weight: 82kg (12st 9lb)
Caps: 20
Points: ....30 (6 tries)

This fly-half is an elusive runner with the ball in hand, thanks partly to his time spent playing rugby sevens. Capable of operating at full-back or fly-half, Rodrigo Fernández has played the latter more recently and become a key part of this Chile side. He shot to fame in 2022 after scoring a stunning solo try against USA. Picking the ball up deep in his half, on a pitch soaked by lashing rain, Fernández weaved his way through the USA defence to score. Fernández duly won the International Rugby Players Men's Try of the Year award for 2022 for his exploits.

"I knew we would win in the United States, I had a lot of faith in winning there," Lemoine said.

"If we were still in the game in the last 20 minutes, with good reserves, we would break them."

Chile were given a hero's welcome on their return to the country and, even more importantly, Sports Minister Alexandra Benado confirmed plans were in motion to redevelop Chile's high-performance centre. World Rugby funding for the next five years was also secured.

That money is crucial to Chile, as they look to grow as a rugby nation. Lemoine is playing a key part in that process and he has plenty of experience, having done a similar job with Uruguay.

Lemoine led Uruguay to Rugby World Cup 2015, and that came about after he improved their infrastructure. Similar work is now taking place with Chile and the redevelopment of their high-performance centre, in the foothills of the Andes, is an example of that.

The creation of the Súper Liga Americana de Rugby in 2020 has also played a key role. It has given South American clubs a place to compete, with Chile creating their own professional side, Selknam – who reached the final in 2022.

Nearly all of the Chile squad play for Selknam and it gives them a chance to work together on a day-to-day basis.

After reaching France, now the challenge for Chile is to compete against the best sides in the world. It will be a tall order for them, but they have shown under Lemoine that they have the spirit and fight to never back down from a challenge.

"I don't know how many people know the pressure we were under to get here," said Lemoine. "Not qualifying meant that we would not be able to continue growing."

RUGBY WORLD CUP PERFORMANCES

1987 .... Did not play
1991 .... Did not qualify
1995 .... Did not qualify
1999 .... Did not qualify
2003 .... Did not qualify
2007 .... Did not qualify
2011 .... Did not qualify
2015 .... Did not qualify
2019 .... Did not qualify

Donald ends All Blacks' long wait

23 October, 2011: Eden Park, Auckland

At the start of Rugby World Cup 2011, fly-half Stephen Donald had been enjoying himself on a fishing holiday. By the end of the tournament, he was on the pitch and kicking New Zealand to glory. It was a remarkable moment for the fly-half, who was drafted into the squad during the tournament as the All Blacks were hit by a string of injuries. First Dan Carter went down in the pool stage, before Colin Slade and Aaron Cruden joined him on the sidelines. That left the door open for Donald to be the most unlikely of heroes, with his penalty in the final proving to be decisive as New Zealand beat France 8-7. After 24 years, the All Blacks were world champions again.

Right: Donald had been on holiday when the tournament started but came in as injury cover.

RUGBY
WORLD CUP
2011
adidas

10

THE STARS TO WATCH

From the very first Rugby World Cup in 1987, players have been using the stage as an opportunity to showcase their talent. Heroes have been born and supporters have been wowed by the likes of Jonah Lomu and Jonny Wilkinson. Now, the latest generation are looking to make their mark in France as the best players in the world assemble. It promises to be a special occasion and everyone involved will be desperate to make history.

Left: Antoine Dupont has established himself as one of the most exciting players to watch.

Emiliano Boffelli

Since making his debut for Argentina in 2017, Emiliano Boffelli has gone on to establish himself as one of the most talented players in the world. Capable of playing in multiple positions in the backline, he is excellent under the high ball and equally adept at offloading in the tackle. His accuracy from the kicking tee makes him the complete package.

FACTS AND FIGURES

Born: .... 16 January, 1995, Santa Fe, Argentina
Position: .... Full-back; wing; centre
Club: .... Edinburgh (SCO)
Height: 1.90m (6ft 3in)
Weight: 91kg (14st 5lb)
Caps: 50
Debut: .... v England in San Juan on 10 June, 2017
Points: .... 249 (12 tries)

From the moment he was walking, Emiliano Boffelli can remember having a rugby ball in his hands. The full-back was born and grew up in the city of Rosario, which is renowned in Argentina for its love of rugby. Boffelli was no different and, with his family being huge fans of the sport, it was not long before he was eventually playing for local team Duendes.

Big things were expected of Boffelli, who had shown he could play multiple positions in the backline, and it was no surprise that he played at various youth levels for Argentina. After suffering a serious knee injury playing for Super Rugby side the Jaguares in 2016, Boffelli had to wait a year to make his Argentina debut. That came in 2017 against England and, all things considered, he has never looked back since then. Boffelli was nominated for World Rugby's Breakthrough Player of the Year at the end of that 12 months, with New Zealand wing Rieko Ioane just pipping him to the award.

However, Boffelli had announced his arrival and his importance to Argentina has only grown. He was a regular for them at full-back at Rugby World Cup 2019, but he can play on the wing or at centre, too.

Boffelli's performances during the tournament in Japan earned him a move to French side Racing 92 before he joined Edinburgh in 2021. He has proved a hit in Scotland, winning Players' Player of the Season in his debut campaign.

The full-back is the complete player, as he is strong in the tackle but fast in attack. He has become a talisman for Argentina thanks to his accurate goal-kicking and he scored 20 points as Los Pumas famously beat New Zealand 25-18 in 2022. Boffelli will have his sights set on more triumphs in France.

Above: Emiliano Boffelli has become one of the most accurate goal-kickers around.

Faf de Klerk

A blonde bundle of energy, Faf de Klerk has made a name for himself ever since he came onto the international scene back in 2016. The scrum-half may be small in size, but his speed around the pitch makes him a nightmare to defend against. Add to that his pinpoint box-kicking and you can see why de Klerk has been successful.

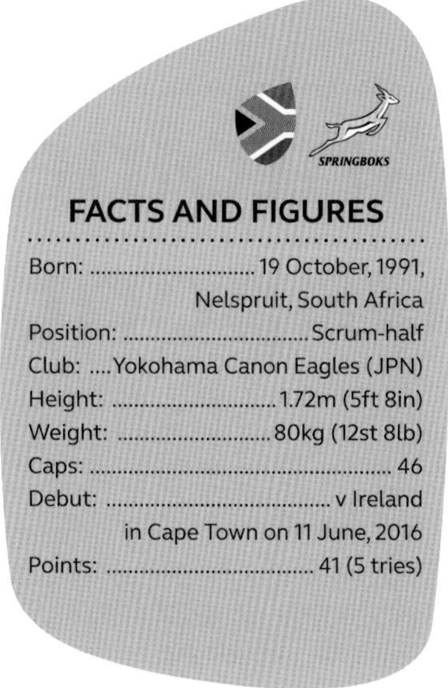

FACTS AND FIGURES

Born: .... 19 October, 1991, Nelspruit, South Africa
Position: .... Scrum-half
Club: ....Yokohama Canon Eagles (JPN)
Height: 1.72m (5ft 8in)
Weight: 80kg (12st 8lb)
Caps: 46
Debut: .... v Ireland in Cape Town on 11 June, 2016
Points: .... 41 (5 tries)

The disappointment at Sale Sharks when it was confirmed in June 2022 Faf de Klerk would be leaving the club tells you all you need to know about the scrum-half. After five years in Manchester, de Klerk had become a cult hero due to his performances on the pitch and the entertaining brand of rugby he brought to Sale. "He likes to look good, no doubt. He never looks more coiffured than he does on game day," Alex Sanderson, Sale's director of rugby, told the *Daily Mail*. "But if you think that's all he is; all show and no go, you get lulled into a false sense of security that maybe you can take him on around the ruck or scrum, and he smashes you. He's a lot tougher than he might appear."

De Klerk has been proving people wrong his whole career, ever since the very start when he missed out on a contract with Super Rugby side the Bulls. The scrum-half did not let that knock him and, after being offered a bursary at the University of Johannesburg, he eventually made it to Super Rugby in 2014 with the Golden Lions.

Two years later, South Africa came calling and de Klerk made his debut during a test series against Ireland. His speed around the park was all too evident to everyone watching, as was his tenacity, with the scrum-half proving a real nuisance at the breakdown.

After moving to play his club rugby in England in 2017, de Klerk feared his international career would stall due to selection criteria around the number of caps players had won. That was scrapped in 2018, though, and just 12 months later de Klerk was starting in a Rugby World Cup final, playing a key role as South Africa went all the way in Japan.

Above: Faf de Klerk is one of the most entertaining scrum-halves around.

Antoine Dupont

The poster boy of French rugby, Antoine Dupont heads to Rugby World Cup 2023 as arguably the biggest star of the entire tournament. That tag, however, is fully justified, as since the last Rugby World Cup he has taken his game to a new level. Dupont was crowned World Rugby Men's 15s Player of the Year in 2021 to cap off a brilliant 12 months.

FACTS AND FIGURES

Born:	15 November, 1996, Lannemezan, France
Position:	Scrum-half
Club:	Stade Toulousain (FRA)
Height:	1.74m (5ft 9in)
Weight:	85kg (13st 3lb)
Caps:	45
Debut:	v Italy in Rome on 11 March, 2017
Points:	60 (12 tries)

As hosts of Rugby World Cup 2023, there is pressure on France to deliver. And no more heavily does that pressure weigh than on the shoulders of scrum-half Antoine Dupont, who has become the leading light for the revolution in French rugby since the last Rugby World Cup. France chose to blood youth after that tournament, opting for an entertaining brand of rugby, and Dupont has been at the heart of it.

His speed and ability to know what support lines to run makes him so dangerous in attack, while he has an offload game that few players can rival. Simply put, Dupont brings energy, and his skill at raising the tempo of a match is what makes him one of the best players on the planet.

The scrum-half was tipped for the top at a young age, but it was at the World Rugby U20 Championship in 2016 where he really caught the eye. Despite France finishing ninth, Dupont scored five tries; he then made his senior debut a year later.

As the years have gone by, Dupont has become more integral for France, and since the last Rugby World Cup he has become irreplaceable in their team. Dupont was named Player of the Six Nations in 2020 and 2022, helping France win the Grand Slam in the latter of those two championships. He was also named World Rugby Men's 15s Player of the Year in 2021 and that rounded off a 12-month period in which Dupont was at the peak of his powers. He helped France beat New Zealand 40-25, while at club level Dupont shone as Toulouse won the Champions Cup and French Top 14 double.

Dupont will have eyes on adding the Webb Ellis Cup to his already growing trophy cabinet, and he will take some stopping.

Above: Antoine Dupont has helped revolutionise how France play rugby.

Tadhg Furlong

Since making his debut, Tadhg Furlong has transformed the role of a prop in rugby. Dynamic and skilful, Furlong has an all-round game that makes him dangerous in attack and solid in defence. Despite enjoying popping up out wide, he is still steady in the scrum and can be effective at the breakdown, too.

FACTS AND FIGURES

Born: .... 14 November, 1992, Wexford, Ireland
Position: .... Prop
Club: .... Leinster (IRE)
Height: 1.85m (6ft 1in)
Weight: 125kg (19st 9lb)
Caps: .... 63 (+7 Lions)
Debut: .... v Wales in Dublin on 29 August, 2015
Points: .... 25 (5 tries)

It was early on during Leinster's Champions Cup semi-final against Toulouse in 2022 that Tadhg Furlong received the ball in midfield. He had men outside him and the obvious conclusion would be that the prop would swiftly pass the ball on as Leinster looked to attack. Instead, however, Furlong threw a huge miss-pass right into the hands of Hugo Keenan and after the game fly-half Johnny Sexton could not help but smile. "I'm sure it will be part of his new highlights reel and there will be speculation now if he could play 12 for Ireland and is he the best playmaker that we have and all that," said Sexton. The reality is that Furlong would have the kind of highlight reel that would make most backs jealous, never mind fellow props.

During the 2021 Six Nations, a clip of Furlong went viral as he sidestepped two Scotland defenders, one of which was fly-half Finn Russell. That is just the way Furlong plays, though, and ever since he came onto the scene he has transformed what is expected from a prop. Traditionally props have been famed for their ability in the scrum; however, Furlong is much more than that. He is dynamic in the loose and he often roams the wide channels, where he can attack and utilise his offloading skills. Furlong's handling abilities are so good he is regularly used in Ireland's backline moves.

Despite his love of attacking, Furlong does not shirk his defensive work and he has become a solid scrummager.

His rise has been recognised, with the Irish prop being named in the World Rugby Men's 15s Dream Team of the Year in 2021. If Ireland are to go far at Rugby World Cup 2023, then Furlong will have a big role to play.

Above: Tadhg Furlong has changed what is expected from a prop.

Rieko Ioane

From an early age, it was clear that Rieko Ioane had all the talent needed to be one of the best players in the world. He burst onto the scene on the wing before the last Rugby World Cup, but he has now developed his game as a centre. France could be Ioane's moment to really shine.

ALL BLACKS

FACTS AND FIGURES

Born: .... 18 March, 1997, Auckland, New Zealand
Position: .... Centre, wing
Club: .... Blues (NZL)
Height: 1.89m (6ft 2in)
Weight: 103kg (16st 3lb)
Caps: 59
Debut: .... v Italy in Rome on 12 November, 2016
Points: ....165 points (33 tries)

Building up to Rugby World Cup 2019, the stage had looked set for Rieko Ioane to be a star of the tournament. After making his debut for the New Zealand Sevens team as a 17-year-old, Ioane was called up to the All Blacks test side a year later. He eventually made his debut at the age of 19, becoming the eighth-youngest All Blacks test debutant, and he marked the occasion by scoring a try. Ioane's career took off from there and, particularly in 2017, it felt like the sky was the limit for this precocious young talent.

Ioane impressed for Super Rugby side the Blues against the British and Irish Lions, helping them win 22-16, and was duly picked to start the first test. He was equally impressive there, scoring two tries and announcing himself to the wider world. His stellar 2017 continued by him finishing as top try scorer in the Rugby Championship and winning World Rugby's Breakthrough Player of the Year. Such was Ioane's form that he was also nominated for World Rugby Men's 15s Player of the Year, but fellow All Black Beauden Barrett pipped him to it.

After finishing top try scorer again in the 2018 Rugby Championship, Ioane looked set to shine at Rugby World Cup the following year. Injuries and a loss of form, however, saw him lose his place, but he has regained it since then by excelling as a centre.

"In 2019 Ioane had a calf injury that kept him out for the early part of the international season, and by the time he was coming right it was the end of the World Cup," said New Zealand head coach Ian Foster in 2021. "He just was not fast in 2019 – he is fast now. He has got his speed back, and got that little swagger that he is pretty proud of."

Above: Ioane broke onto the scene as a winger for the All Blacks.

Marika Koroibete

After making the switch from Rugby League to union in 2017, Marika Koroibete has gone on to make more than 50 test appearances for the Wallabies. The wing is now undoubtedly one of the most deadly finishers on the planet and he will be vital to Australia's chances of success at Rugby World Cup 2023.

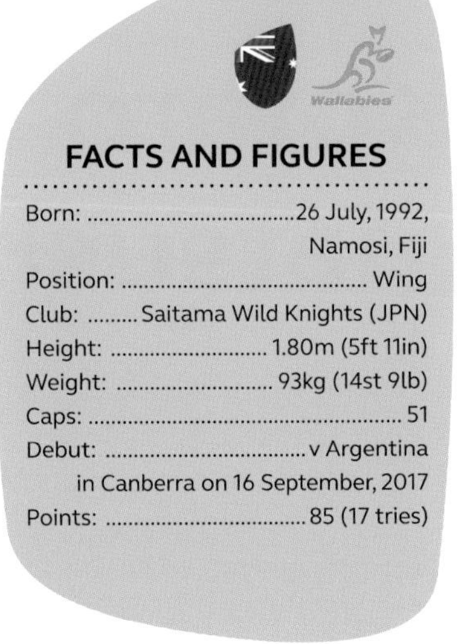

FACTS AND FIGURES

Born: ....26 July, 1992, Namosi, Fiji
Position: .... Wing
Club: .... Saitama Wild Knights (JPN)
Height: 1.80m (5ft 11in)
Weight: 93kg (14st 9lb)
Caps: 51
Debut: .... v Argentina in Canberra on 16 September, 2017
Points: .... 85 (17 tries)

It comes as little surprise to learn that growing up Marika Koroibete used to idolise Fiji wing Rupeni Caucaunibuca. A young Koroibete used to watch Caucaunibuca in Rugby World Cups of the late 1990s and early 2000s, dreaming of following in his footsteps. The pair both come from villages in Fiji and the similarities in their games are clear, with Koroibete following Caucaunibuca's lead of being a destructive ball-carrier.

Koroibete's path to the top has not been straightforward, though, and he first moved to Australia in 2011 to pursue a career in Rugby League. He proved a hit in the sport, but elected to switch codes in 2017 as he eyed making his mark for the Wallabies.

Koroibete has proved a hit. He is not the biggest player, but he possesses incredible power and his speed around the pitch makes him so dangerous in attack. The Australia coaching staff, however, have been most impressed by his work ethic, and he has developed into one of the game's toughest tacklers.

"If we kick a ball, he is at full pace chasing, he is concrete when he hits, his work ethic is phenomenal, I have not seen another winger like it," said former Australia coach Dave Rennie.

Koroibete is one of Australia's most important weapons in attack, as he often comes in off his wing to create havoc in the midfield. He has an uncanny knack of evading the first defender and Australia fly-half Noah Lolesio admits he is a joy to have outside him in the backline: "He is a freak. I am just happy that I am one of his teammates, not opposing him," Lolesio said in 2022. "I reckon he is the best winger in the world." Koroibete will be out to prove his teammate right at Rugby World Cup 2023.

Above: Koroibete has become a hit after switching from Rugby League in 2017.

Kotaro Matsushima

After lighting up Rugby World Cup 2019, Kotaro Matsushima is hungry to make his mark once again on the biggest stage of all. The wing is blessed with lightning pace and is one of the best finishers around. If Japan are to pull off more heroics in France, then Matsushima will undoubtedly play a part.

FACTS AND FIGURES

Born: ....26 February, 1993, Pretoria, South Africa
Position: .... Wing, full-back
Club: .... Tokyo Sungoliath (JPN)
Height: 1.78m (5ft 10in)
Weight: 88kg (13st 12lb)
Caps: 46
Debut: .... v Philippines in Manila on 3 May, 2014
Points: .... 110 (22 tries)

It was after Kotaro Matsushima's stunning hat-trick in the opening game of Rugby World Cup 2019 that Japan head coach Jamie Joseph compared him to a Ferrari. "If we can create opps (opportunities) then both of our wingers, they can finish," said Joseph. "They will get accolades for the tries because that is what the Ferraris get on the outside."

Rugby World Cup 2019 was Matsushima's breakout moment and he became a star in Japan during the tournament. The hosts were crying out for a poster boy to take centre stage, and Matsushima did that by scoring five tries as Japan made the quarter-finals for the first time in their history. There were plenty of good performers in that Japan team, but flying wing Matsushima was the most eye-catching. His pace and ability to beat defenders got fans off their seats and it was no surprise that he earned a move to French club ASM Clermont Auvergne in 2020 off the back of Rugby World Cup.

The winger impressed at his new club, most notably with yet another hat-trick – this time against Bristol Bears in the Champions Cup – and Matsushima believes that playing in France has developed his game. He is a star in Japan now, but his rugby journey began back in South Africa. Matsushima was born there to a Japanese mother and eventually enrolled in the Sharks academy in Durban. The wing went on to play club rugby in South Africa, Australia and France but is now playing in Japan once more. That is ideal for Japan, as they step up their preparations for Rugby World Cup 2023. Joseph has described Matsushima as a player with "an X-factor" and there is a sense he could once again light up the whole tournament.

Above: Kotaro Matsushima turned out to be a star of Rugby World Cup 2019.

Semi Radradra

Fiji may have been eliminated in the pool stage of Rugby World Cup 2019, but Semi Radradra made a lasting impact on the tournament. The Fijian, who can operate at centre or wing, terrorised defences and, even in defeat to Wales, was named player of the match. Now, he's ready for more action in France.

FLYING FIJIANS

FACTS AND FIGURES

Born: 13 June, 1992, Taveuni, Fiji
Position: Wing, centre
Club: Bristol Bears (ENG)
Height: 1.88m (6ft 2in)
Weight: 105kg (16st 7lb)
Caps: 11
Debut: v Georgia in Suva on 16 June, 2018
Points: 25 (5 tries)

For Semi Radradra, it was a single photograph that changed his life and got the ball rolling for his magical career. Radradra, who began his life working in the gold mines of Fiji, was playing for the country's under-20 side when scouts from Australian Rugby League side Parramatta Eels saw a photo of him. They were blown away by the youngster's size and encouraged him to try his hand at switching codes. It proved to be a masterstroke, with Radradra scoring 82 tries in 94 appearances, as he tormented defences in the Australian National Rugby League.

The Fijian was given the nickname "Semi-Trailer", which relates to a pick-up truck, due to his size and power. In 2017 French side Rugby Club Toulonnais persuaded him to return to rugby union and, just 62 seconds into his debut, Radradra scored a try with his first touch of the ball.

By Rugby World Cup 2019 there was a huge buzz around Radradra, and he showed just why by excelling in Japan. Against Georgia he scored two tries and set up three, running 177 metres and beating 11 defenders. It was against Wales, though, that Radradra really caught the eye. Despite Fiji losing 29-17, the wing was in sparkling form and the Wales defence struggled to handle him. "It was one of the best displays I have seen and I am talking as a fan," said England head coach Eddie Jones. "Just to be at the World Cup is a humbling experience to see him play with such power, pace and guile."

Since then, Radradra has moved to English club Bristol Bears, making the Premiership Team of the Season in his first year. He also helped Fiji win the gold medal in rugby sevens at the Tokyo Olympics in 2021. People are now rightfully wondering, is there anything Radradra cannot do?

Above: Semi Radradra was a big hit for Fiji at Rugby World Cup 2019.

Marcus Smith

England have had their eye on Marcus Smith ever since he was first making waves playing school rugby for Brighton College. The fly-half eventually made his debut for England in 2021 and he has gone on to impress on the international stage. The sky is the limit for Smith and 2023 feels like just the start.

England Rugby

FACTS AND FIGURES

Born: ....14 February, 1999, Makati City, Philippines
Position: ....Fly-half
Club: .... Harlequins (ENG)
Height: 1.75m (5ft 9in)
Weight: 82kg (12st 13lb)
Caps: 20
Debut: .... v USA in Twickenham on 4 July, 2021
Points: ....156 (7 tries)

Marcus Smith was just seven years old when he first started playing rugby. Back then he was living in Singapore, after his parents had moved there from the Philippines, and even at that early age his talent was obvious.

After his family moved to England when he was 13, Smith was beginning to show real promise, and he duly earned a sports scholarship to Brighton College. As he progressed up the age ranks, the buzz around Smith grew. He eventually finished his time at Brighton College by captaining them to an unbeaten season and then just a year later he was training with England. That was in 2017, when head coach Eddie Jones invited Smith down as England were training in Brighton. Smith was able to get a feel for what life could be like in an England shirt and four years later he was making his test debut.

In between then, the fly-half showed why he has long been tipped for the top. He made his debut for Harlequins during the 2017-18 season at the age of 18, becoming the second-youngest Premiership debutant ever. During that season he scored 179 points in 26 appearances and won Harlequins Players' Player of the Season, Supporters' Player of the Season and the Nick Duncombe Young Player of the Season.

Smith was the top points scorer in the 2020-21 season, as he fired Harlequins to the Premiership, and he was called up to the British and Irish Lions squad as a result. He has since established himself as one of England's best fly-halves and former coach Eddie Jones tipped him for the top. "There is no ceiling to how good he can be," said Jones during the 2022 Six Nations. "If he keeps on wanting to get better and keeps having a learning mindset, then he could be an outstanding player at test level by the World Cup."

Above: Marcus Smith has been tipped for the top ever since he was a teenager.

Louis Rees-Zammit

By the age of 20, Louis Rees-Zammit had already achieved so much. He had made his Wales debut, won the Six Nations and even toured with the British and Irish Lions. Now, "Rees Lightning" is ready to make his mark at Rugby World Cup 2023, as he continues his meteoric rise.

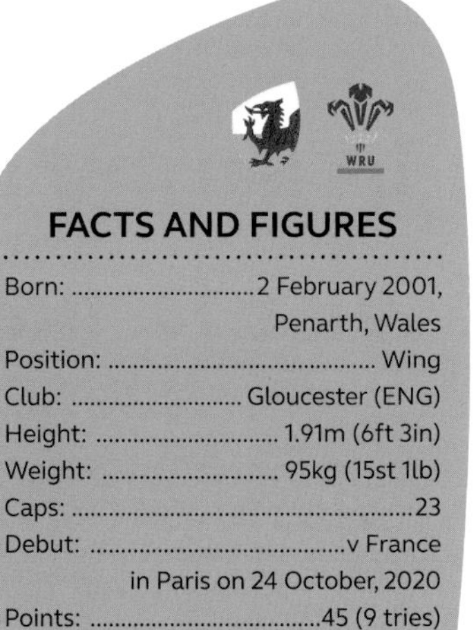

FACTS AND FIGURES

Born: ....2 February 2001, Penarth, Wales
Position: .... Wing
Club: .... Gloucester (ENG)
Height: 1.91m (6ft 3in)
Weight: 95kg (15st 1lb)
Caps: 23
Debut: ....v France in Paris on 24 October, 2020
Points: ....45 (9 tries)

Louis Rees-Zammit had barely turned 18 when Gloucester decided he was ready to make his Premiership debut for them. It was a bold call from the English club, but very quickly it became clear that Rees-Zammit was ready for the big time. Rees-Zammit made his Premiership debut in April 2019 and the following season he was fully blooded into the first team.

The winger took little time to make an impact and by December he was making history, becoming the first 18-year-old to score a hat-trick in the English top flight. Rees-Zammit eventually finished that debut season with 10 tries in the Premiership, only one off the top scorer.

Unsurprisingly, the wing's form had caught the attention of Wales and, just under a year after making his Premiership debut, he was playing for them in the Six Nations. Rees-Zammit has proved to be a hit in international rugby too, scoring four tries as Wales won the 2021 Six Nations. In the wake of that he received a call-up for the British and Irish Lions tour to South Africa. The wing was still only 20 then and he became the youngest player on the day of selection in a touring party since David Hewitt in 1959. There were flashes of brilliance from Rees-Zammit during that tour, mainly against provincial sides, while the squad affectionately had him shave a lightning bolt into his hair in honour of his nickname.

So far "Rees Lightning" has lived up to his billing and now he will get the chance to make his mark at a Rugby World Cup. Wales have had great wings in recent history, such as George North and Shane Williams, and Rees-Zammit looks ready to follow in their footsteps.

Above: Louis Rees-Zammit is one of the fastest wings in the game.

Uruguay down flying Fijians

23 September, 2019: Kamaishi Recovery Memorial Stadium, Kamaishi

It had been 16 years since Uruguay had won a Rugby World Cup match and, as such, they arrived in Japan fuelled more by hope than expectation. In their opening game, however, they ended their long wait for a victory as they defeated Fiji in a thrilling encounter. Despite losing to Australia, Fiji had impressed in their opening game of the tournament. They made 12 changes for this Uruguay encounter, though, and ultimately they paid the price. Fiji were unquestionably sloppy, but Uruguay were impressive, too, as they matched their opponents physically. Tries from Santiago Arata, Manuel Diana and Juan Manuel Cat, and 15 points from the boot of fly-half Felipe Berchesi, secured the win for Uruguay on what was an historic day for the country.

Right: Uruguay's win over Fiji was an historic day for the country.

21
20
ISC

RUGBY
WORLD CUP
2003

RUGBY WORLD CUP HISTORY

Nothing compares to the drama of a Rugby World Cup and, ever since the first tournament in 1987, fans have witnessed plenty of memorable moments. With each passing year, the quality of rugby on show goes up a level and France promises to be the latest thrilling instalment in what has been a captivating story. Four different countries have got their hands on the famous Webb Ellis Cup so far, but rugby has been the real winner.

Left: Martin Johnson and England conquered all in 2003, as the country won its first men's Rugby World Cup.

Rugby World Cup 1987

New Zealand and Australia

This opening Rugby World Cup set the tone for future tournaments, as it was packed with drama and entertainment. Hosts Australia and New Zealand looked destined to meet in the final, but France and flying full-back Serge Blanco put paid to that. The French, however, were no match for the All Blacks, who became the very first Rugby World Cup winners.

Right from the start of this tournament, New Zealand showed they meant business as they finished top of their pool thanks to some brilliant, attacking rugby. Scrum-half David Kirk marshalled the backline superbly, with the likes of Craig Green and John Kirwan excelling outside him. In total, the All Blacks scored 190 points on their way to topping Pool 3, with Fiji finishing in second place behind them to also reach the quarter-finals.

Fellow hosts Australia also caught the eye in the pool stage, as they too finished first and with a 100 per cent record. After a tight opening win against England, who finished second in Pool 1, the Wallabies saw off USA and Japan, and already people were speculating about them facing the All Blacks in the final.

Wales also finished with a 100 per cent record in the pool stage. They snuck past Ireland 13-6 in their opening game and then beat Canada and Tonga to make a dream start in the first-ever Rugby World Cup.

Pool 4 gave everyone a taste of what was to come, though, as France topped it thanks to the brilliance of full-back Serge Blanco. He scored 12 points as Les Bleus drew 20-20 with Scotland and, as both sides beat Romania and Zimbabwe, France claimed top spot in the pool due to them having a superior points difference. They continued their good form in the quarter-finals, beating Fiji, and that would earn them a semi-final showdown with Australia.

The Wallabies, and in particular fly-half Michael Lynagh, were beginning to find their groove, and a 33-15 win over Ireland underlined their credentials to go all the way.

On the other side of the draw, the All Blacks looked in imperious form, conceding just three points and scoring 30 as they saw off Scotland in their quarter-final. That set up a semi-final with Wales, who stunned England 16-3 in Brisbane. Wales' run ended in the next round, however, as New Zealand ran in eight tries during a 49-6 victory that booked them a place in the first-ever Rugby World Cup final.

The other semi-final proved to be much closer, though, as Australia and France played out a Rugby World Cup classic in Sydney. Australia led the match three times, but France kept coming back. In the dying moments the

RUGBY WORLD CUP HEROES

JOHN KIRWAN (New Zealand)

New Zealand has a rich history of brilliant wings and John Kirwan certainly goes down as one of their greats after his performance at Rugby World Cup 1987. He was in stunning form at the tournament, finishing as the joint top try scorer alongside teammate Craig Green, who also managed six tries. Crucially, Kirwan delivered when the All Blacks needed him most, as he scored two tries in the semi-final and one in the final, too.

scores were tied at 24-24 and extra-time was looming, before full-back Blanco finished off a stunning team move, which went through the hands of 11 players, to score the winning try. It was heartbreak for Australia, who had the added agony of then losing the bronze final by one point to Wales.

After beating the Wallabies, France were dreaming of pulling off one more shock by defeating New Zealand in the final. The French, however, like everyone else, were simply no match for New Zealand, as the All Blacks put in another strong display to win 29-9.

Right: Serge Blanco's try for France against hosts Australia in the semi-finals remains one of the most iconic moments in rugby history.

TOURNAMENT STATISTICS

Host nations: New Zealand and Australia
Dates: 22 May-20 June, 1987
Teams: 16
Matches: 32
Overall attendance: 448,318

POOL 1	W	D	L	PF	PA	Pts
Australia	3	0	0	108	4	6
England	2	0	1	100	32	4
USA	1	0	2	39	99	2
Japan	0	0	3	48	123	0

POOL 2	W	D	L	PF	PA	Pts
Wales	3	0	0	82	31	6
Ireland	2	0	1	84	41	4
Canada	1	0	2	65	90	2
Tonga	0	0	3	29	98	0

POOL 3	W	D	L	PF	PA	Pts
New Zealand	3	0	0	190	34	6
Fiji	1	0	2	56	101	2
Italy	1	0	2	40	110	2
Argentina	1	0	2	49	90	2

POOL 4	W	D	L	PF	PA	Pts
France	2	1	0	145	44	5
Scotland	2	1	0	135	69	5
Romania	1	0	2	61	130	2
Zimbabwe	0	0	3	53	151	0

QUARTER-FINALS

New Zealand	30-3	Scotland
Australia	33-15	Ireland
France	31-16	Fiji
Wales	16-3	England

SEMI-FINALS

France	30-24	Australia
New Zealand	49-6	Wales

BRONZE FINAL

Wales	22-21	Australia

THE FINAL

New Zealand	29-9	France

	NEW ZEALAND	FRANCE
T:	Jones, Kirk, Kirwan	Berbizier
C:	Fox	Camberabero
P:	Fox 4	Camberabero
DG:	Fox	

LEADING POINTS SCORERS

1. Grant Fox (NZL) **126**
2. Michael Lynagh (AUS) **82**
3. Gavin Hastings (SCO) **62**

LEADING TRY SCORERS

1. Craig Green (NZL) **6**
2. John Kirwan (NZL) **6**
3. Matt Burke (AUS) **5**

= Mike Harrison (ENG) **5**
= John Gallagher (NZL) **5**
= Alan Whetton (NZL) **5**
= David Kirk (NZL) **5**

Rugby World Cup 1991
UK, Ireland and France

After narrowly missing out on glory at Rugby World Cup 1987, Australia were determined to go all the way this time around. They achieved their dream by beating England in the final during a tournament that was full of shocks. Western Samoa made the quarter-finals and their performances underlined how the game of rugby was growing around the world.

After finishing third at the first Rugby World Cup, it was expected that Wales would be contenders to go all the way in 1991 – particularly as the tournament was taking place on home soil for them. They were, however, stunned in the opening match of Rugby World Cup 1991, as Western Samoa beat them 16-13 in front of 45,000 fans in Cardiff. It was a result that sent shockwaves through the rest of the teams at the tournament and Western Samoa followed it up by narrowly losing 9-3 to Australia.

Even with that defeat, Western Samoa finished second in Pool 3 behind the Wallabies, with Wales eliminated before the knockout stage.

Western Samoa were joined in the quarter-finals by another emerging rugby nation, as Canada finished second in Pool 4 behind France.

The growing strength in depth of competing nations was clear to see and Japan were buoyed by claiming their first-ever Rugby World Cup win by beating Zimbabwe. They still had to settle for going out in the pool stage, though, with Scotland and Ireland finishing ahead of them, but the victory gave them confidence going forward.

In Pool 1, New Zealand maintained their 100 per cent record at Rugby World Cups as they beat England and pipped them to top spot. The reigning champions looked lethal once again and their victory over Canada in the quarter-finals underlined their superiority as they scored five tries. Waiting for them in the semi-finals would be Australia, who snuck past hosts Ireland by a solitary point.

On the other side of the draw, England were quietly going about their business, and a 19-10 win over France in Paris had them believing this could be their year.

The prospect of Australia facing New Zealand in the semi-finals was exciting, but equally mouth-watering was that of England going head-to-head with Scotland. That came about after the Scots defeated Western Samoa, who had become one of the stars of the tournament following their win against Wales.

England versus Scotland proved to be a cagey affair, with neither side scoring a try. In the end, England edged it 9-6 in front of a devastated Murrayfield crowd.

The other semi-final proved to be just as competitive, as Australia and New

RUGBY WORLD CUP HEROES

MICHAEL LYNAGH (Australia)

After impressing at the very first Rugby World Cup in 1987, Michael Lynagh continued his fine form four years later as Australia went all the way. Lynagh expertly marshalled the Wallabies' backline from fly-half, while he also played an important leadership role as vice-captain. Deadly accurate from the kicking tee, Lynagh scored points for Australia in every match at the tournament. Crucially, he scored eight points in the final, as the Wallabies pipped England 12-6.

Zealand played out the latest chapter of their growing rivalry. The All Blacks had never lost a Rugby World Cup game, but that statistic was broken as the Wallabies defeated them 16-6, thanks to tries from David Campese and Tim Horan.

Now all eyes were on Twickenham, with England looking to lift the Webb Ellis Cup in their own backyard. Confidence was high in their camp, but Australia edged them in what proved to be another tight encounter. Prop Tony Daly scored the only try of the game, as the trusty boot of Michael Lynagh ensured the Wallabies claimed a 12-6 victory. It was despair for England, who had come so close – but they would have their revenge in the future.

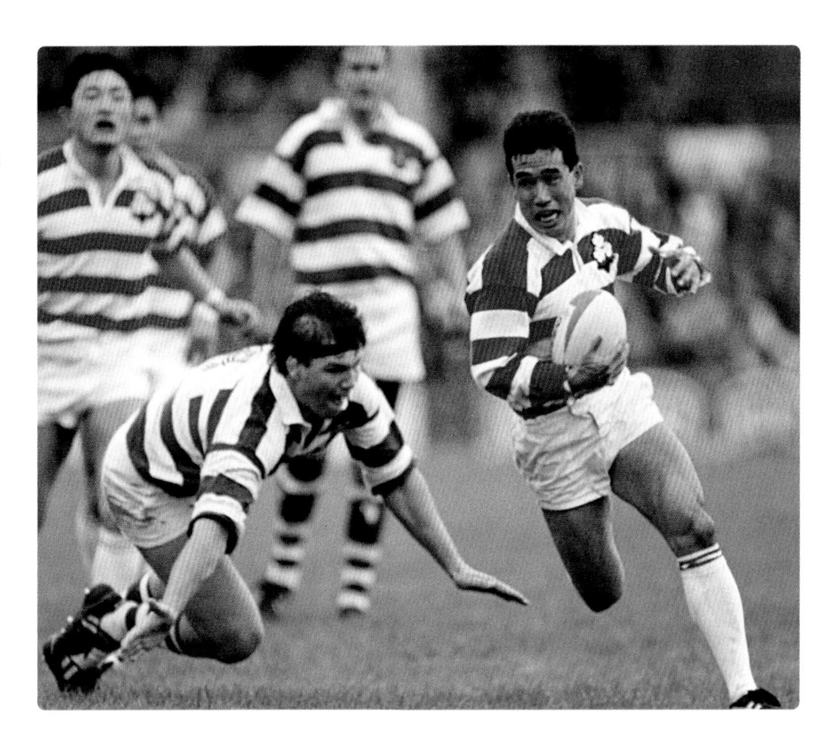

Right: Japan secured their first-ever Rugby World Cup win in 1991, as they defeated Zimbabwe.

TOURNAMENT STATISTICS

Host nations: England, France, Ireland, Scotland and Wales

Dates: 3 October-2 November, 1991

Teams: 16 (33 during qualifying)

Matches: 32

Overall attendance: 1,060,065

POOL A	W	D	L	PF	PA	Pts
New Zealand	3	0	0	95	39	6
England	2	0	1	85	33	4
Italy	1	0	2	57	76	2
USA	0	0	3	24	113	0

POOL B	W	D	L	PF	PA	Pts
Scotland	3	0	0	122	36	6
Ireland	2	0	1	102	51	4
Japan	1	0	2	77	87	2
Zimbabwe	0	0	3	31	158	0

POOL C	W	D	L	PF	PA	Pts
Australia	3	0	0	79	25	6
Western Samoa	2	0	1	54	34	4
Wales	1	0	2	32	61	2
Argentina	0	0	3	38	83	0

POOL D	W	D	L	PF	PA	Pts
France	3	0	0	82	25	6
Canada	2	0	1	45	33	4
Romania	1	0	2	31	64	2
Fiji	0	0	3	27	63	0

QUARTER-FINALS

England	19-10	France
Scotland	28-6	Western Samoa
Australia	19-18	Ireland
New Zealand	29-13	Canada

SEMI-FINALS

England	9-6	Scotland
Australia	16-6	New Zealand

BRONZE FINAL

New Zealand	13-6	Scotland

THE FINAL

Australia	12-6	England

	AUSTRALIA	ENGLAND
T:	Daly	
C:	Lynagh	
P:	Lynagh (2)	Webb (2)

LEADING POINTS SCORERS

1. Ralph Keyes (IRE) **68**
2. Michael Lynagh (AUS) **66**
3. Gavin Hastings (SCO) **61**

LEADING TRY SCORERS

1. David Campese (AUS) **6**
= Jean-Baptiste Lafond (FRA) **6**
3. Tim Horan (AUS) **4**
= Brian Robinson (IRE) **4**
= Iwan Tukalo (SCO) **4**
= Rory Underwood (ENG) **4**

Rugby World Cup 1995

South Africa

If ever a tournament highlighted the power of rugby, then it was Rugby World Cup 1995. The tournament united host nation South Africa, who had been re-admitted to international rugby in 1992 after apartheid was abolished. The Springboks' Rugby World Cup debut proved to be memorable, as they stunned everyone by going all the way.

From the very first game of Rugby World Cup 1995, the tone was set for what would turn out to be a very memorable tournament. South Africa went into that opening match as tournament hosts and were making their Rugby World Cup debut against Australia, who were the reigning champions and unbeaten over the course of the previous year. Few expected the Springboks to topple the Wallabies, but they ran out 27-18 winners in Cape Town, thanks largely to 22 points from fly-half Joel Stransky. South Africa would go on to top Pool A, claiming wins over Canada and Romania too, with Australia having to settle for second.

South Africa impressed in the pool stage, but there were plenty of other sides showing that they were contenders to go all the way. New Zealand, who had the powerful wing Jonah Lomu in their ranks, stormed to the top of Pool C, finishing ahead of Ireland and scoring 222 points in just three games.

England and France enjoyed perfect starts to the tournament and were joined in the quarter-finals by Scotland and Western Samoa, with the latter looking to improve upon their strong showing at Rugby World Cup 1991. Once again, however, Western Samoa came unstuck in the knockout stage, as South Africa defeated them 42-14. Their reward for that would be a showdown with France in the semi-finals after they beat Ireland 36-12, with fly-half Thierry Lacroix kicking 26 of those points.

On the other side of the draw, New Zealand and Lomu were continuing to look unstoppable, running in six tries as they beat Scotland 48-30. Lomu scored only one of those, but it was in the semi-finals where he really made a name for himself. The All Blacks were facing England, who had defeated Australia 25-22 thanks to a late Rob Andrew drop goal to send the reigning champions home early. Now the hope was that England could reach the final, but they were blown away by Lomu. The wing scored four tries during a 49-25 victory for New Zealand, with England defenders simply unable to deal with his physicality.

Waiting for the All Blacks in the final was South Africa, who had squeezed past France 19-15 in the semi-finals thanks to Ruben Kruger's solitary

RUGBY WORLD CUP HEROES

FRANCOIS PIENAAR (South Africa)

Behind every great team is a great captain – and Francois Pienaar certainly falls into that category. The flanker often led by example, throwing himself into tackles and rucks to set the tone for the rest of his teammates. Pienaar rose to the occasion at Rugby World Cup 1995, as he proved to be a unifying figure both on and off the field, and the image of him receiving the Webb Ellis Cup from Nelson Mandela is iconic in sport.

try. All the talk before the game was about New Zealand's attacking threat – particularly that of Lomu and Marc Ellis – who had both scored seven tries at the tournament. What followed, however, was a tight game, as both sides' defences excelled and instead points came from the boots of Andrew Mehrtens and Joel Stransky. With the match tied at 9-9 it went to extra-time, with Stransky eventually slotting a winning drop goal as South Africa claimed a 15-12 win.

President Nelson Mandela, famously wearing a Springbok jersey, then handed the Webb Ellis Cup to South Africa captain Francois Pienaar in a moment that will always live on.

Right: New Zealand wing Jonah Lomu proved to be an unstoppable force throughout Rugby World Cup 1995.

TOURNAMENT STATISTICS

Host nation: South Africa
Dates: 5 May-24 June, 1995
Teams: 16 (52 during qualifying)
Matches: 32
Overall attendance: 936,900

POOL A	W	D	L	PF	PA	Pts
South Africa	3	0	0	68	26	6
Australia	2	0	1	87	41	4
Canada	1	0	2	45	50	2
Romania	0	0	3	14	97	0

POOL B	W	D	L	PF	PA	Pts
England	3	0	0	95	60	6
Western Samoa	2	0	1	96	88	4
Italy	1	0	2	69	94	2
Argentina	0	0	3	69	87	0

POOL C	W	D	L	PF	PA	Pts
New Zealand	3	0	0	222	45	6
Ireland	2	0	1	93	94	4
Wales	1	0	2	89	68	2
Japan	0	0	3	55	252	0

POOL D	W	D	L	PF	PA	Pts
France	3	0	0	114	47	6
Scotland	2	0	1	149	27	4
Tonga	1	0	2	44	90	2
Ivory Coast	0	0	3	29	172	0

QUARTER-FINALS

France	36-12	Ireland
South Africa	42-14	Western Samoa
England	25-22	Australia
New Zealand	48-30	Scotland

SEMI-FINALS

South Africa	19-15	France
New Zealand	45-29	England

BRONZE FINAL

France	19-9	England

THE FINAL

South Africa	15-12 AET	New Zealand

	SOUTH AFRICA	NEW ZEALAND
P:	Stransky (3)	Mehrtens (3)
DG:	Stransky (2)	Mehrtens

LEADING POINTS SCORERS

1. Thierry Lacroix (FRA) **112**
2. Gavin Hastings (SCO) **104**
3. Andrew Mehrtens (NZL) **84**

LEADING TRY SCORERS

1. Marc Ellis (NZL) **7**
= Jonah Lomu (NZL) **7**
3. Gavin Hastings (SCO) **5**
= Rory Underwood (ENG) **5**

Rugby World Cup 1999
Wales

With the number of teams competing at a Rugby World Cup increased to 20, the 1999 edition of the tournament promised to be bigger and better than ever before. Rugby had also moved into the professional era, and the depth of talent across the globe was now being seen. Wales were the hosts of this tournament, but once again the southern hemisphere reigned supreme, as Australia were crowned champions.

A familiar theme of the opening three Rugby World Cups was the southern hemisphere nations' dominance at the tournaments. New Zealand, Australia and South Africa had each won one of the opening Rugby World Cups, and they started the 1999 edition suggesting that once again one of them would go all the way.

All three nations won their pools to advance to the quarter-finals, taking advantage of the new format for the tournament. With 20 teams at Rugby World Cup 1999, five pools of four were drawn and the top team from each one was guaranteed a quarter-final berth. The five runners-up and the best third-placed team would face an extra game in the quarter-final play-offs. Australia, New Zealand and South Africa avoided that by winning their pools and were joined in the quarter-finals by France and hosts Wales.

England, Fiji, Ireland, Samoa and Scotland finished as runners-up and were joined in the play-offs by Argentina, who had been third in Wales' pool. Despite coming third, Argentina had looked impressive and had finished level on points with Wales and Samoa ahead of them. They continued their good form in the play-offs, stunning Ireland 28-24. Scotland navigated their way past Samoa, while England gave a glimpse of the future as Jonny Wilkinson kicked them to victory against Fiji.

England came unstuck in the next round, though, as they were defeated 44-21 by reigning champions South Africa. Fly-half Jannie de Beer was the star of the show with five drop goals and England undertook a reboot after the tournament to build towards Rugby World Cup 2003.

Australia and New Zealand joined the Springboks in the semi-finals, underlining the southern hemisphere nations' dominance. Scrum-half George Gregan scored two tries as the Wallabies beat Wales, and Jonah Lomu, who would finish as the tournament's top try scorer, continued his rise by helping New Zealand win 30-18 against Scotland.

France completed the semi-final line-up by beating Argentina in Dublin, but it was expected they would suffer against the All Blacks in the next round. Lomu was once again in fine form, scoring two tries; however, it was not enough, as a

RUGBY WORLD CUP HEROES

JOHN EALES (Australia)

Rugby World Cup 1999 proved to be the crowning moment of a glittering career for John Eales. The second-row captained Australia to glory and for the second time in his career got his hands on the famous Webb Ellis Cup. Eales was an impressive forward, who was strong in defence but mobile in attack and blessed with good hands. He was also an accomplished goal-kicker. Tactically astute, he is one of Australia's most successful captains ever.

spirited France side ran in four tries of their own to win 43-31 at Twickenham.

The other semi-final was a complete contrast, with both Australia and South Africa failing to score a try. Instead, it became a battle of the boot and Australia's Matt Burke was the hero as the Wallabies won 27-21 after extra-time.

South Africa bounced back to win the bronze final and then all eyes were on the showdown between Australia and France. After impressing in the semi-final, it was thought France could win their first-ever Rugby World Cup, but Australia had too much for them. Ben Tune and Owen Finegan scored tries, while Burke was deadly from the kicking tee again, as the Wallabies won 35-12.

Right: France stunned New Zealand with a thrilling victory in the semi-finals.

TOURNAMENT STATISTICS

Host nation: Wales
Dates: 1 October-6 November, 1999
Teams: 20 (65 during qualifying)
Matches: 41
Overall attendance: 1,556,572

POOL A	W	D	L	PF	PA	Pts
South Africa	3	0	0	132	35	6
Scotland	2	0	1	120	58	4
Uruguay	1	0	2	42	97	2
Spain	0	0	3	81	22	0

POOL B	W	D	L	PF	PA	Pts
New Zealand	3	0	0	176	28	6
England	2	0	1	184	47	4
Tonga	1	0	2	47	171	2
Italy	0	0,	3	35	196	0

POOL C	W	D	L	PF	PA	Pts
France	3	0	0	108	52	6
Fiji	2	0	1	124	68	4
Canada	1	0	2	114	82	2
Namibia	0	0	3	42	186	0

POOL D	W	D	L	PF	PA	Pts
Wales	2	0	1	118	71	4
Samoa	2	0	1	97	72	4
Argentina	2	0	1	83	51	4
Japan	0	0	3	36	40	0

POOL E	W	D	L	PF	PA	Pts
Australia	3	0	0	135	31	6
Ireland	2	0	1	100	45	4
Romania	1	0	2	50	126	2
USA	0	0	3	52	135	0

QUARTER-FINAL PLAY-OFFS

England	45-24	Fiji
Scotland	35-20	Samoa
Argentina	28-24	Ireland

QUARTER-FINALS

Australia	24-9	Wales
South Africa	44-21	England
New Zealand	30-18	Scotland
France	47-26	Argentina

SEMI-FINALS

Australia	27-21 (aet)	South Africa
France	43-31	New Zealand

BRONZE FINAL

South Africa	22-18	New Zealand

THE FINAL

Australia	35-12	France

	AUSTRALIA	FRANCE
T:	Tune, Finegan	
C:	Burke (2)	
P:	Burke (7)	Lamaison (4)

LEADING POINTS SCORERS

1. Gonzalo Quesada (ARG) **102**
2. Matt Burke (AUS) **101**
3. Jannie de Beer (RSA) **97**

LEADING TRY SCORERS

1. Jonah Lomu (NZL) **8**
2. Jeff Wilson (NZL) **6**
3. Keith Wood (IRE) **4**
= Philippe Bernat-Salles (FRA) **4**
= Viliame Satala (FIJ) **4**
= Dan Luger (ENG) **4**

Rugby World Cup 2003

Australia

Australia went into Rugby World Cup 2003 as the hosts and reigning champions. As a result, plenty of people were wondering if the Wallabies could retain the Webb Ellis Cup. England, however, had developed into a dangerous team under Clive Woodward and they were full of belief that they could become the first northern hemisphere nation to go all the way.

Having arrived in Australia as one of the favourites to win Rugby World Cup 2003, the pressure was on England to deliver. Under head coach Clive Woodward, the team had improved immensely since the 1999 tournament and they set their stall out by impressing in the pool stage. England won all four of their matches, which included a 25-6 victory over South Africa, and that vitally meant they topped Pool C and avoided a quarter-final showdown with New Zealand. The All Blacks had looked typically ominous on the way to topping Pool D, scoring 282 points in four games and pipping Wales to first place.

New Zealand were not the only side to enjoy a 100 per cent record during the pool stage, with Australia and France managing the same as well. The Wallabies topped Pool A ahead of Ireland and their four victories included a 142-0 win over Namibia, in which they scored 22 tries. France scored more than 200 points during their four victories, which secured them top spot in Pool B ahead of Scotland. Les Bleus were particularly impressive against the Scots, who they defeated 51-9 and scored five tries against.

It all made for some intriguing quarter-finals, with New Zealand and South Africa the first to kick things off. The All Blacks swept the Springboks aside 29-9 and their backs, such as wing Joe Rokocoko, looked the part in another fine performance.

Australia would join them in the semi-finals, as the hosts continued to make steady progress. They defeated Scotland and Elton Flatley was proving to be a vital weapon for the Wallabies, with the centre kicking more than half of his side's points on the way to a 33-16 win.

On the other side of the draw, England and France progressed to the semi-finals. Les Bleus continued to look impressive, with Frédéric Michalak the star of the show as they beat Ireland 43-21 in the quarter-finals. England made harder work of their encounter against Wales, though, and they were trailing at half-time before coming back to win 28-17.

Two mouthwatering semi-finals were up next between some of rugby's great rivals. England took on France, and a kicking masterclass from Jonny Wilkinson saw him score all of his side's points en route to a 24-7 win. That

RUGBY WORLD CUP HEROES

JONNY WILKINSON (England)

In the build-up to Rugby World Cup 2003, all the talk was around Jonny Wilkinson. The fly-half had become the poster boy of English rugby and the pressure was on him to deliver. Wilkinson stepped up to the plate in Australia, as he excelled during the tournament. He is a legend of English rugby, with his last-minute drop goal to win the final regarded as one of the most iconic moments in Rugby World Cup history.

would set up a showdown with hosts Australia, who defeated the All Blacks thanks to a brilliant performance from their kicker, Flatley.

Given their form throughout the tournament, the final was billed as being a battle between the kicking boots of Flatley and Wilkinson. It proved to be that way, with both sides only managing one try each, as Lote Tuqiri scored for the Wallabies and Jason Robinson for England. The two sides then traded blows through their kickers and, with the game tied at the final whistle, it went to extra-time. Eventually, Jonny Wilkinson was the hero, as he slotted a drop goal with seconds to go.

Right: England lived up to their billing of pre-tournament favourites by going all the way.

TOURNAMENT STATISTICS

Host nation: Australia
Dates: 10 October-22 November, 2003
Teams: 20 (80 during qualifying)
Matches: 48
Overall attendance: 1,837,547

POOL A	W	D	L	PF	PA	Pts
Australia	4	0	0	273	32	18
Ireland	3	0	1	41	56	15
Argentina	2	0	2	140	57	11
Romania	1	0	3	65	192	5
Namibia	0	0	4	28	310	0

POOL B	W	D	L	PF	PA	Pts
France	4	0	0	204	70	20
Scotland	3	0	1	102	97	14
Fiji	2	0	2	98	114	10
USA	1	0	3	86	125	6
Japan	0	0	4	79	163	0

POOL C	W	D	L	PF	PA	Pts
England	4	0	0	255	47	19
South Africa	3	0	1	184	60	15
Samoa	2	0	2	138	117	10
Uruguay	1	0	3	56	255	4
Georgia	0	0	4	46	200	0

POOL D	W	D	L	PF	PA	Pts
New Zealand	4	0	0	282	57	20
Wales	3	0	1	132	98	14
Italy	2	0	2	77	123	8
Canada	1	0	3	54	135	5
Tonga	0	0	4	46	178	1

QUARTER-FINALS

New Zealand	29-9	South Africa
Australia	33-16	Scotland
France	43-21	Ireland
England	28-17	Wales

SEMI-FINALS

Australia	22-10	New Zealand
England	24-7	France

BRONZE FINAL

New Zealand	40-13	France

THE FINAL

England	20-17 (aet)	Australia

	ENGLAND	AUSTRALIA
T:	Robinson	Tuqiri
P:	Wilkinson (4)	Flatley (4)
DG:	Wilkinson	

LEADING POINTS SCORERS

1. Jonny Wilkinson (ENG) **113**
2. Frédéric Michalak (FRA) **103**
3. Elton Flatley (AUS) **100**

LEADING TRY SCORERS

1. Doug Howlett (NZL) **7**
= Mils Muliaina (NZL) **7**
3. Joe Rokocoko (NZL) **6**

Rugby World Cup 2007

France

Rugby World Cup 2007 proved to be a tournament full of shocks and surprises. Argentina set the tone by stunning hosts France in the opening game, but the likes of Fiji joined the party as well. In the end, South Africa were too much for the rest of the competition and went all the way to get their hands on a second Webb Ellis Cup.

The tone for Rugby World Cup 2007 was set from the very first match of the tournament. Hosts France went into the opening game against Argentina looking to lay down a marker, but they were stunned in Paris and fell to a 17-12 defeat. Los Pumas were worthy winners too, putting in a performance full of defensive resilience and heart to underline how much they had developed over recent years.

They continued their fine form throughout the pool stage and, after beating Ireland as well, they topped Pool D with a perfect record. Ireland, having lost to France, were on the plane home and Rugby World Cup 2007 had its first major casualty.

There was plenty more drama to come, though, not least in Pool A, where reigning champions England were beaten 36-0 by South Africa in their opening game. The Springboks would go on to top the pool and England had to settle for second.

The shocks kept coming as Pool B threw up yet more upsets. Australia claimed top spot with a perfect record; however, they were joined in the quarter-finals by Fiji. That came about as Fiji won a thrilling game against Wales 38-34, with both sides playing some brilliant attacking rugby.

Pool C was the only one in which upsets were kept to a minimum. New Zealand topped it with four wins, scoring more than 300 points in the process, while Scotland pipped Italy to second place.

The drama returned in the quarter-finals, however, as France beat New Zealand. The All Blacks had never failed to make the semi-finals of a Rugby World Cup before, but tries from Thierry Dusautoir and Yannick Jauzion sent them home early.

Argentina's brilliant run showed no signs of slowing down, though, as they beat Scotland 19-13 to reach the final four. They were joined there by England and South Africa, who both claimed good wins. The Springboks defeated Fiji 37-20, while England edged Australia 12-10 during a tight game down in Marseille.

England and France met in the semi-finals and both sides were relieved to have made it there having suffered defeats in their opening games of the tournament. Their encounter proved to be a close game, with Josh Lewsey's

RUGBY WORLD CUP HEROES

BRYAN HABANA (South Africa)

There have been plenty of wings who have lit up Rugby World Cups and Bryan Habana certainly did that in 2007. Blessed with incredible speed, he proved a nightmare for defenders throughout the tournament. Habana eventually finished as the tournament's top try scorer with eight and he was vital in South Africa going all the way. Habana enjoyed a glittering career and, along with Jonah Lomu, he has the most tries in men's Rugby World Cup history.

second-minute try the only one of the game. Jonny Wilkinson, as he so often was, proved to be England's hero, as he kicked them to a 14-9 win.

In the other semi-final South Africa clicked into gear, scoring four tries and beating Argentina 37-13. It looked like Los Pumas had run out of steam, but they dismissed that by recovering to beat France 34-10 in the bronze final.

The final saw a rematch between England and South Africa. The Springboks had been comfortable winners in the pool stage, but the final was a tight affair. Neither side was able to score a try, but it was South Africa who held their nerve to win 15-6.

Right: Argentina stunned the world when they beat France in the opening game of the tournament.

TOURNAMENT STATISTICS

Host nation: France
Dates: 7 September-20 October, 2007
Teams: 20 (91 during qualifying)
Matches: 48
Overall attendance: 2,245,731

POOL A	W	D	L	PF	PA	Pts
South Africa	4	0	0	189	47	19
England	3	0	1	108	88	14
Tonga	2	0	2	89	96	9
Samoa	1	0	3	69	143	5
USA	0	0	4	61	142	1

POOL B	W	D	L	PF	PA	Pts
Australia	4	0	0	215	41	20
Fiji	3	0	1	114	136	15
Wales	2	0	2	168	105	12
Japan	0	1	3	64	210	3
Canada	0	1	3	51	210	2

POOL C	W	D	L	PF	PA	Pts
New Zealand	4	0	0	309	35	20
Scotland	3	0	1	116	66	14
Italy	2	0	2	85	117	9
Romania	1	0	3	40	161	5
Portugal	0	0	4	38	209	1

POOL D	W	D	L	PF	PA	Pts
Argentina	4	0	0	143	33	18
France	3	0	1	188	37	15
Ireland	2	0	2	64	82	9
Georgia	1	0	3	50	111	5
Namibia	0	0	4	30	212	0

QUARTER-FINALS

England	12-10	Australia
France	20-18	New Zealand
South Africa	37-20	Fiji
Argentina	19-13	Scotland

SEMI-FINALS

England	14-9	France
South Africa	37-13	Argentina

BRONZE FINAL

Argentina	34-10	France

THE FINAL

South Africa	15-6	England

SOUTH AFRICA	**ENGLAND**
P: Steyn, Montgomery (4)	Wilkinson (2)

LEADING POINTS SCORERS

1. Percy Montgomery (RSA) **105**
2. Felipe Contepomi (ARG) **91**
3. Jonny Wilkinson (ENG) **67**

LEADING TRY SCORERS

1. Bryan Habana (RSA) **8**
2. Drew Mitchell (AUS) **7**
3. Doug Howlett (NZL) **6**

= Shane Williams (WAL) **6**

Rugby World Cup 2011

New Zealand

After suffering their worst-ever performance at a Rugby World Cup in 2007, New Zealand were out to go all the way as hosts of the tournament. The All Blacks had to cope with plenty of hurdles along the way, including injuries in key positions, but they kept their cool to lift the Webb Ellis Cup for the first time in 24 years.

The pressure was on New Zealand like never before at Rugby World Cup 2011. Not only were the All Blacks hosts of the tournament, but they had also not lifted the Webb Ellis Cup since the inaugural competition back in 1987.

After crashing out in the quarter-finals in 2007, New Zealand were keen to start fast, and they topped Pool A with a 100 per cent record. That included an impressive 37-17 win over France, but their joy was dampened by injury problems. Before the final pool game against Canada, fly-half Dan Carter suffered a groin injury that meant he was out for the rest of the tournament, and captain Richie McCaw had to miss the match too with a foot issue.

New Zealand was not the only nation looking to make amends at Rugby World Cup 2011. After going out in the pool stage four years before, Ireland wanted to prove a point and they did that by topping Pool C ahead of Australia.

Elsewhere, Argentina picked up where they left off from Rugby World Cup 2007 by once again qualifying for the quarter-finals. They came second in Pool B behind England, with Scotland sent home early.

Reigning champions South Africa and Wales completed the quarter-final line-up, with the latter coming second in Pool D after a decisive 17-10 win over Samoa.

After several expected results in the pool stage, the quarter-finals threw up some shocks. Australia and Wales had both come second in their pools, but they improved in the knockout stages to reach the semi-finals.

Australia stunned reigning champions South Africa 11-9, while Wales impressed against Ireland and scored three tries en route to a 22-10 win. France and New Zealand maintained their perfect records, though, to reach the final four. France defeated England 19-12, while New Zealand claimed a 33-10 win over Argentina. After losing Carter to injury, the All Blacks were relieved McCaw was able to nurse a foot issue and play. However, their problems continued as Carter's replacement, Colin Slade, became the latest player to be hit by injury. In his absence scrum-half Piri Weepu stepped up to kick seven penalties and steady the ship.

Weepu was on form again in the semi-finals, scoring 12 points as the All Blacks

RUGBY WORLD CUP HEROES

RICHIE McCAW (New Zealand)

There are few players who can boast as glittering a CV as Richie McCaw. The flanker is undoubtedly a New Zealand legend and he captained the All Blacks to two Rugby World Cups. The first of those was in 2011 and, despite being dogged by a foot injury, McCaw led New Zealand well. His fighting spirit, particularly at the breakdown, embodied the All Blacks' hunger to get their hands back on the Webb Ellis Cup.

beat Australia 20-6 to reach the final. They were joined there by France, who snuck past Wales 9-8 after the Welsh had played nearly 60 minutes with 14 men following a red card for captain Sam Warburton.

New Zealand were looking to finish the job now they were in the final, but once again they were struck by injury at fly-half. Aaron Cruden, who had filled in for Slade, was the unlucky victim, as he came off just over 30 minutes into the final. It meant it was down to emergency call-up Stephen Donald to deliver. He had been on holiday at the start of tournament, but he ended it by kicking the decisive penalty as New Zealand beat France 8-7.

Right: Wales and captain Sam Warburton suffered semi-final heartbreak at the hands of France.

TOURNAMENT STATISTICS

Host nation: New Zealand
Dates: 9 September-23 October, 2011
Teams: 20 (91 during qualifying)
Matches: 48
Overall attendance: 1,477,294

POOL A	W	D	L	PF	PA	Pts
New Zealand	4	0	0	240	49	20
France	2	0	2	124	96	11
Tonga	2	0	2	80	98	9
Canada	1	1	2	82	168	6
Japan	0	1	3	69	184	2

POOL B	W	D	L	PF	PA	Pts
England	4	0	0	137	34,	18
Argentina	3	0	1	90	40	14
Scotland	2	0	2	73	59	11
Georgia	1	0	3	48	90	4
Romania	0	0	4	44	169	0

POOL C	W	D	L	PF	PA	Pts
Ireland	4	0	0	135	34	17
Australia	3	0	1	173	48	15
Italy	2	0	2	92	95	10
USA	1	0	3	38	122	4
Russia	0	0	4	57	196	1

POOL D	W	D	L	PF	PA	Pts
South Africa	4	0	0	166	24	18
Wales	3	0	1	180	34	15
Samoa	2	0	2	91	49	10
Fiji	1	0	3	59	167	5
Namibia	0	0	4	44	266	0

QUARTER-FINALS

Wales	22-10	Ireland
France	19-12	England
Australia	11-9	South Africa
New Zealand	33-10	Argentina

SEMI-FINALS

France	9-8	Wales
New Zealand	20-6	Australia

BRONZE FINAL

Australia	21-18	Wales

THE FINAL

New Zealand	8-7	France

	NEW ZEALAND	FRANCE
T:	Woodcock	Dusautoir
C:		Trinh-Duc
P:	Donald	

LEADING POINTS SCORERS

1. Morné Steyn (RSA) **62**
2. James O'Connor (AUS) **52**
3. Kurt Morath (TGA) **45**

LEADING TRY SCORERS

1. Chris Ashton (ENG) **6**
= Vincent Clerc (FRA) **6**
3. Adam Ashley-Cooper (AUS) **5**
= Keith Earls (IRE) **5**
= Israel Dagg (NZL) **5**

Rugby World Cup 2015

England

As hosts of Rugby World Cup 2015, England were dreaming about getting their hands on the Webb Ellis Cup. However, it was New Zealand who went all the way, as they became the first team to win back-to-back Rugby World Cups. The tournament in England proved to be a memorable one, with plenty of drama and shocks.

The pressure was on England to deliver at Rugby World Cup 2015. As hosts of the tournament they were backed by huge support and there was also a sense of unfinished business after a quarter-final exit in 2011.

England got off to a steady start, defeating Fiji in their opening game, but things quickly unravelled from there. First, they were stunned by Wales at Twickenham. Fly-half Dan Biggar put in a stunning performance, scoring 23 points, and Wales claimed a famous 28-25 victory.

Just days later, England were defeated again and this time they could have no complaints. Australia's attack was at its best to cut them open and they secured a 33-13 win that ended England's time in the tournament. For the first time in Rugby World Cup history, the hosts of a tournament had failed to get out of their pool.

There were shocks elsewhere, though, as Japan beat two-time world champions South Africa. Japan wing Karne Hesketh scored a last-minute try as they ran out 34-32 winners. South Africa recovered to top Pool B and Japan narrowly missed out on a quarter-final berth to Scotland, who came second.

There were no bumps in the road for reigning champions New Zealand, however, who topped Pool C ahead of Argentina with four wins. In the final pool, Ireland looked in imperious form as they won all their games to finish ahead of France.

France had not looked at their best and were sent home in the quarter-finals after a devastating performance from New Zealand. The All Blacks scored nine tries during the win and underlined why they were favourites to go all the way. They were joined in the semi-finals by South Africa, who edged past Wales thanks to the boot of Handré Pollard. If that game was tight, it had nothing on Australia and Scotland's encounter, as the Wallabies won by a solitary point thanks to Bernard Foley's last-gasp penalty.

Argentina completed the semi-final line-up thanks to a brilliant 43-20 win over Ireland. It meant that the final four sides in the competition were all from the southern hemisphere. Los Pumas came unstuck in the next round, however, as Australia beat them 29-15. The Wallabies had been written off

RUGBY WORLD CUP HEROES

DAN CARTER (New Zealand)

Dan Carter arrived at Rugby World Cup 2015 with a point to prove. The fly-half had cruelly had his tournament cut short by injury four years earlier and he was keen to not let this moment pass him by. Carter duly delivered and was in brilliant form throughout Rugby World Cup 2015, both from the kicking tee and with ball in hand. He shone in the final, scoring 19 points as New Zealand were crowned world champions.

before the tournament, but a brilliant hat-trick from Adam Ashley-Cooper booked them a spot in the final. There they would meet New Zealand, who edged South Africa in an enthralling clash at Twickenham. South Africa fly-half Pollard was once again lethal from the kicking tee, but the All Blacks secured a 20-18 win.

The Springboks bounced back with a 24-13 win in the bronze final and then it was all eyes on Twickenham for Australia and New Zealand's showdown.

The All Blacks were looking to become the first team to retain the Webb Ellis Cup and they thrived under the pressure. Dan Carter, who had missed the 2011 final through injury, shone and scored 19 points in a 34-17 win.

Right: New Zealand wing Julian Savea was the top try scorer at Rugby World Cup 2015.

TOURNAMENT STATISTICS

Host nation: England
Dates: 18 September-31 October, 2015
Teams: 20 (96 during qualifying)
Matches: 48
Overall attendance: 2,477,805

POOL A	W	D	L	PF	PA	Pts
Australia	4	0	0	141	35	17
Wales	3	0	1	111	62	13
England	2	0	2	133	75	11
Fiji	1	0	3	84	101	5
Uruguay	0	0	4	30	226	0

POOL B	W	D	L	PF	PA	Pts
South Africa	3	0	1	176	56	16
Scotland	3	0	1	136	93	14
Japan	3	0	1	98	100	12
Samoa	1	0	3	69	124	6
USA	0	0	4	50	156	0

POOL C	W	D	L	PF	PA	Pts
New Zealand	4	0	0	174	49	19
Argentina	3	0	1	179	70	15
Georgia	2	0	2	53	123	8
Tonga	1	0	3	70	130	6
Namibia	0	0	4	70	174	1

POOL D	W	D	L	PF	PA	Pts
Ireland	4	0	0	134	35	18
France	3	0	1	120	63	14
Italy	2	0	2	74	88	10
Romania	1	0	3	60	129	4
Canada	0	0	4	58	131	2

QUARTER-FINALS

South Africa	23-19	Wales
New Zealand	62-13	France
Ireland	20-43	Argentina
Australia	35-34	Scotland

SEMI-FINALS

South Africa	18-20	New Zealand
Argentina	15-29	Australia

BRONZE FINAL

South Africa	24-13	Argentina

THE FINAL

New Zealand	34-17	Australia

	NEW ZEALAND	FRANCE
T:	Milner-Skudder, Nonu, Barrett	Pocock, Kuridrani
C:	Carter (2)	Foley (2)
P:	Carter (4)	Foley
DG:	Carter	

LEADING POINTS SCORERS

1. Nicolás Sánchez (ARG) **97**
2. Handré Pollard (RSA) **93**
3. Bernard Foley (AUS) **82**

= Dan Carter (NZL) **82**

LEADING TRY SCORERS

1. Julian Savea (NZL) **8**
2. Nehe Milner-Skudder (NZL) **6**
3. Bryan Habana (RSA) **5**

= Gareth Davies (WAL) **5**
= Juan Imhoff (ARG) **5**
= JP Pietersen (RSA) **5**

Rugby World Cup 2019

Japan

Rugby World Cup's first-ever visit to Asia proved to be a huge success, as fans flocked to Japan for the tournament. The hosts delivered under pressure, enjoying their best-ever tournament by reaching the quarter-finals, but in the end it was South Africa who conquered all to get their hands on the Webb Ellis Cup once again.

Rugby World Cup 2019 started with a bang – and that energy and passion refused to fizzle out throughout the whole tournament. Japan lit up the competition in the opening game, beating Russia 30-10 as winger Kotaro Matsushima became the first Japanese player to score a hat-trick at a Rugby World Cup. Japan carried that momentum all the way through the pool stage, beating both Ireland and Scotland on the way to four wins from as many games.

Hosts Japan's fine form set the tone for the tournament and ensured the whole country got caught up in Rugby World Cup fever.

The other pools were showcasing high-class action too, and New Zealand topped Pool B ahead of South Africa. Their final pool game was cancelled due to Typhoon Hagibis and that impacted Pool C as well, with England and France's decider to see who would finish top unable to take place. As it was, England claimed top spot ahead of France and were joined in the quarter-finals by Wales and Australia. Wales won Pool D and looked in impressive form, with the side enjoying a 100 per cent record in the pool stage thanks largely to a hard-fought 29-25 defeat of the Wallabies.

Wales continued their good form in the quarter-finals, with Ross Moriarty scoring a late try to secure a 20-19 win over France. That proved to be the closest of the quarter-finals, as England scored four tries on their way to a 40-16 victory against Australia. New Zealand put in a dominant display against Ireland, scoring seven tries, and Japan's dream tournament ended at the hands of South Africa.

The Springboks had gone into Rugby World Cup 2019 under the radar, but they were growing with every game at the tournament and emerging as contenders. Standing in their way in the semi-finals was Wales and they snuck past them 19-16 thanks to a 76th-minute penalty from fly-half Handré Pollard.

The other semi-final proved to be just as tight as England came up against New Zealand, who were looking to lift the Webb Ellis Cup for a third time in a row. Eddie Jones' side came flying out of the blocks and opened the scoring within two minutes as Manu Tuilagi scored a try. The All Blacks,

RUGBY WORLD CUP HEROES

SIYA KOLISI (South Africa)

No one underlined South Africa's fight and spirit at Rugby World Cup 2019 more than Siya Kolisi. The flanker epitomised the strength and physicality of the Springboks team, particularly in defence, and he shone throughout the tournament. Kolisi led by example, both on and off the pitch, and he is regarded as one of the most iconic South Africa captains. Born in a township outside of Port Elizabeth, his rise to the top has inspired others to follow him.

unsurprisingly, fought back after that, but the boot of George Ford kicked England to a 19-7 win and a first Rugby World Cup final in 12 years.

It was a repeat of that final from 2007, as once again England and South Africa went head-to-head. The game was in the balance at half-time, with South Africa 12-6 ahead after dominating the scrum. After the break, though, the Springboks raised their level and wings Makazole Mapimpi and Cheslin Kolbe both scored tries. Pollard had nerves of steel from the kicking tee too, scoring 22 points, and in the end South Africa were worthy winners.

Right: Japan make history by reaching their first-ever Rugby World Cup quarter-final.

TOURNAMENT STATISTICS

Host nation: .... Japan
Dates: .... 20 September-2 November, 2019
Teams: .... 20 (93 during qualifying)
Matches: 48
Overall attendance: 1,704,443

POOL A	W	D	L	PF	PA	Pts
Japan	4	0	0	115	62	19
Ireland	3	0	1	121	27	16
Scotland	2	0	2	119	55	11
Samoa	1	0	3	58	128	5
Russia	0	0	4	19	160	0

POOL B	W	D	L	PF	PA	Pts
New Zealand	3	1	0	157	22	16
South Africa	3	0	1	185	36	15
Italy	2	0	1	98	78	12
Namibia	0	1	3	34	175	2
Canada	0	1	3	14	177	2

POOL C	W	D	L	PF	PA	Pts
England	3	1	0	119	20	17
France	3	1	0	79	51	15
Argentina	2	0	2	106	91	11
Tonga	1	0	3	67	105	6
USA	0	0	4	52	156	0

POOL D	W	D	L	PF	PA	Pts
Wales	4	0	0	136	69	19
Australia	3	0	1	136	68	16
Fiji	1	0	3	110	108	7
Georgia	1	0	3	65	122	5
Uruguay	1	0	3	60	140	4

QUARTER-FINALS

England	40-16	Australia
New Zealand	46-14	Ireland
Wales	20-19	France
South Africa	26-3	Japan

SEMI-FINALS

England	19-7	New Zealand
South Africa	19-16	Wales

BRONZE FINAL

New Zealand	40-17	Wales

THE FINAL

South Africa	32-12	England

	SOUTH AFRICA	ENGLAND
T:	Mapimpi, Kolbe	
C:	Pollard (2)	
P:	Pollard (6)	Farrell (4)

LEADING POINTS SCORERS

1. Handré Pollard (RSA) **69**
2. Owen Farrell (ENG) **58**
3. Richie Mo'unga (NZL) **54**

LEADING TRY SCORERS

1. Josh Adams (WAL) **7**
2. Makozole Mapimpi (RSA) **6**
3. Kotaro Matsushima (JPN) **5**

Kolisi evokes the spirit of 1995

2 November, 2019: International Stadium Yokohama, Yokohama

Rugby World Cup 1995 is forever etched in history as a tournament that united South Africa and, 24 years on from that, similar feelings were evoked by the Springboks going all the way in Japan. A year out from the tournament, they were not viewed as one of the favourites and Rassie Erasmus was drafted in to take charge. He transformed them into a well-oiled and physical machine, and opposition teams could not cope with their power. Captain Siya Kolisi summed up the strength of South Africa, with the flanker the heartbeat of the team. He led South Africa to Rugby World Cup glory and the photograph of him holding the Webb Ellis Cup aloft in Yokohama has become an iconic image that underlines the power of rugby.

Right: Siya Kolisi lifts the Webb Ellis Cup high into the Tokyo sky after South Africa were crowned champions.

The Webb Ellis Cup
WORLD CUP

RUGBY

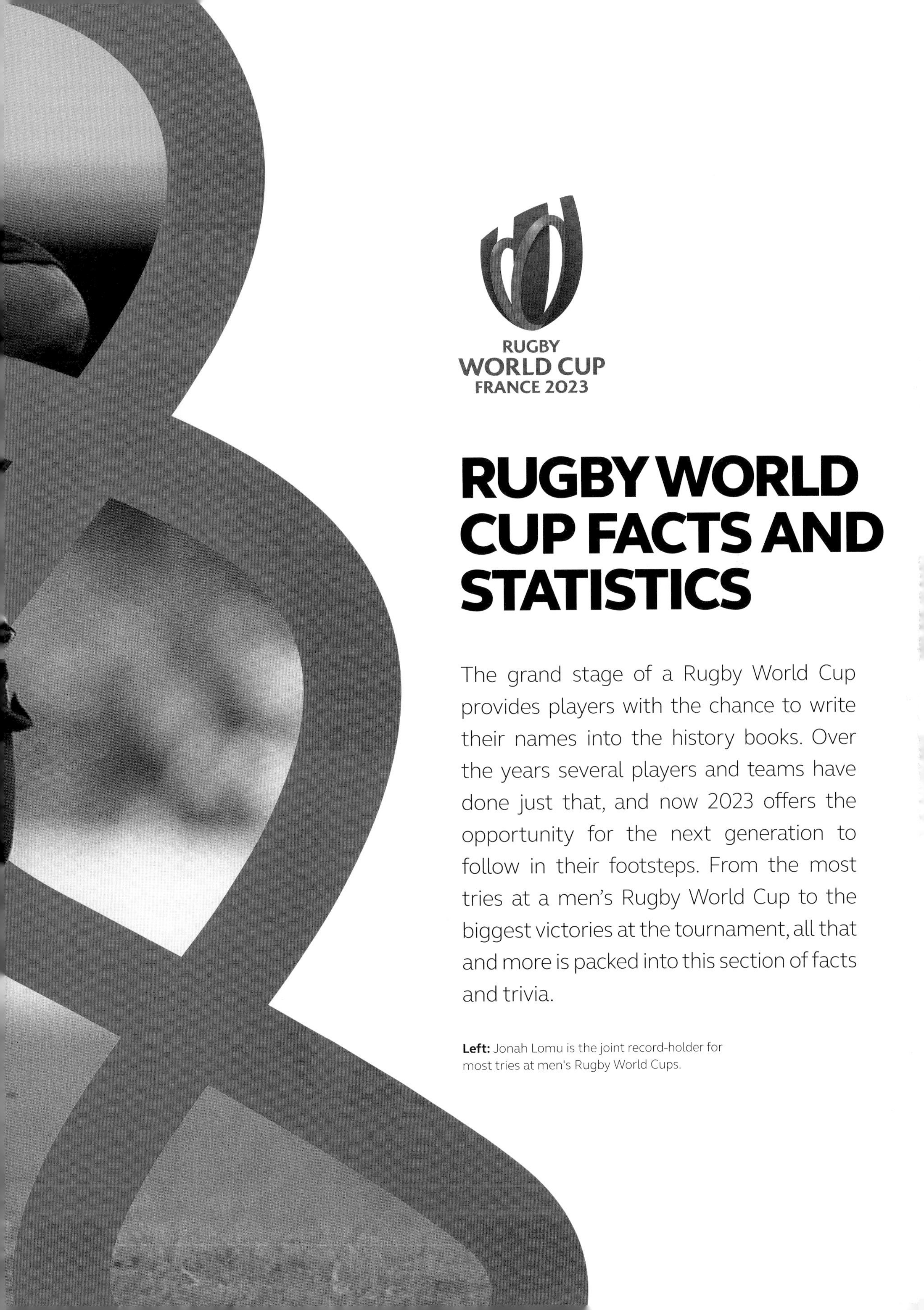

RUGBY WORLD CUP FACTS AND STATISTICS

The grand stage of a Rugby World Cup provides players with the chance to write their names into the history books. Over the years several players and teams have done just that, and now 2023 offers the opportunity for the next generation to follow in their footsteps. From the most tries at a men's Rugby World Cup to the biggest victories at the tournament, all that and more is packed into this section of facts and trivia.

Left: Jonah Lomu is the joint record-holder for most tries at men's Rugby World Cups.

Rugby World Cup facts and stats: Players

TRY-SCORING RECORDS

Most tries overall:

Position, player, country, Rugby World Cup span – tries

1. Bryan Habana, South Africa, 2007-15 – 15 tries
= Jonah Lomu, New Zealand, 1995-99 – 15 tries
3. Drew Mitchell, Australia, 2007-15 – 14 tries
4. Doug Howlett, New Zealand, 2003-07 – 13 tries
5. Adam Ashley-Cooper, Australia, 2011-15 – 12 tries
6. Chris Latham, Australia, 1999-2007 – 11 tries
= Josevata Rokocoko, New Zealand, 2003-07 – 11 tries
= Rory Underwood, England, 1987-95 – 11 tries
= Vincent Clerc, France, 2007-11 – 11 tries
10. Brian Lima, Samoa, 1991-2007 – 10 tries
= David Campese, Australia, 1987-95 – 10 tries
= Shane Williams, Wales, 2003-11 – 10 tries

Leading try scorers by tournament:

(Year, player (country), tries)

1987 Craig Green (NZL) and John Kirwan (NZL) – 6 tries
1991 David Campese (AUS) and Jean-Baptiste Lafond (FRA) – 6 tries
1995 Marc Ellis (NZL) and Jonah Lomu (NZL) – 7 tries
1999 Jonah Lomu (NZL) – 8 tries
2003 Doug Howlett (NZL) and Mils Muliaina (NZL) – 7 tries
2007 Bryan Habana (RSA) – 8 tries
2011 Chris Ashton (ENG) and Vincent Clerc (FRA) – 6 tries
2015 Julian Savea (NZL) – 8 tries
2019 Josh Adams (WAL) – 7 tries

Above: Bryan Habana is the joint record-holder for most tries at men's Rugby World Cups.

Most tries in a match:

6 Marc Ellis (NZL) against Japan in Bloemfontein in 1995

Most tries in a single tournament:

8 Jonah Lomu (NZL) in 1999, Bryan Habana (RSA) in 2007 and Julian Savea (NZL) in 2015

First-ever Rugby World Cup try:

A penalty try for New Zealand against Italy, opening match, 1987.

Most matches played without scoring a try:

22 Jason Leonard (ENG, 1991-2003)

Youngest try scorer:

George North (WAL) was 19 years and 166 days old when he scored two tries against Namibia in New Plymouth on 26 September, 2011.

Oldest try scorer:

Diego Ormaechea (URU) was 40 years and 13 days old when he scored against Spain in Galashiels on 2 October, 1999.

POINTS-SCORING RECORDS

Most points:

Position, points, player (country, Rugby World Cup span)

1. 277, Jonny Wilkinson (ENG, 1999-2011)
2. 227, Gavin Hastings (SCO, 1987-95)
3. 195, Michael Lynagh (AUS, 1987-95)
4. 191, Daniel Carter (NZL, 2007-15)
5. 170, Grant Fox (NZL, 1987-91)
6. 163, Andrew Mehrtens (NZL, 1995-99)
7. 162, Handré Pollard (RSA, 2015-present)
8. 140, Chris Paterson (SCO, 1999-2011)
9. 136, Frédéric Michalak (FRA, 2003-15)
10. 135, Gonzalo Quesada (ARG, 1999-2003)

Above: Jonny Wilkinson's kicking made him one of the best players in Rugby World Cup history.

Most points in a match:
45 Simon Culhane (NZL) against Japan in 1995

Most points in a tournament:
126 Grant Fox (NZL) in 1987

Most penalties:
58 Jonny Wilkinson (ENG)

Most penalties in a match:
8 Matt Burke (AUS) against South Africa in 1999, Gavin Hastings (SCO) against Tonga in 1995, Gonzalo Quesada (ARG) against Samoa in 1999 and Thierry Lacroix against Ireland in 1995

Most penalties in a tournament:
31 Gonzalo Quesada (ARG) in 1991

Most conversions overall:
58 Dan Carter (NZL)

Most conversions in a match:
20 Simon Culhane (NZL) v Japan, 1995

Most conversions in a tournament:
30 Grant Fox (NZL) in 1987

Most drop goals overall:
14 Jonny Wilkinson (ENG)

Most drop goals in a match:
5 Jannie de Beer (RSA) against England in 1999

Most drop goals in a tournament:
8 Jonny Wilkinson (ENG) in 2003

Leading points scorers by tournament:
Year, player (country), points
1987 Grant Fox (NZL), 126
1991 Ralph Keyes (IRE), 68
1995 Thierry Lacroix (FRA), 112
1999 Gonzalo Quesada (ARG), 102
2003 Jonny Wilkinson (ENG), 113
2007 Percy Montgomery (RSA), 105
2011 Morné Steyn (RSA), 62
2015 Nicolás Sánchez (ARG), 97
2019 Handré Pollard (RSA), 69

APPEARANCE RECORDS

Most appearances:
Position, appearances, player (country, span)

1. 22, Jason Leonard (ENG, 1991-2003)
= 22, Richie McCaw (NZL, 2003-15)
3. 21, Alun Wyn Jones (WAL, 2007-present)
4. 20, Schalk Burger (RSA, 2003-15)
= 20, George Gregan (AUS, 1995-2007)
= 20, Keven Mealamu (NZL, 2003-15)
7. Adam Ashley-Cooper (AUS, 2007-19)
= 19, Mike Catt (ENG, 1995-2007)
= 19, Jonny Wilkinson (ENG, 1999-2011)
= 19, Sam Whitelock (NZL, 2011-present)
= 19, Sonny Bill Williams (NZL, 2011-19)

Oldest player:
Diego Ormaechea (URU) was 40 years and 26 days old when he played against South Africa in 1999.

Youngest player:
Vasil Lobzhanidze (GEO) was 18 years and 340 days old when he played against Tonga in 2015.

Youngest player in the final:
Jonah Lomu (NZL) was 20 years and 43 days old when he played against South Africa in the Rugby World Cup 1995 final.

Youngest Rugby World Cup winner:
Francois Steyn (RSA) was 20 years and 159 days old when South Africa won the tournament in 2007.

RUGBY WORLD CUP 2023

POOL A

NEW ZEALAND
FRANCE
ITALY
URUGUAY
NAMIBIA

FRANCE v NEW ZEALAND	Fri, 8 Sept – 21:00	Saint-Denis – Stade de France
ITALY v NAMIBIA	Sat, 9 Sept – 13:00	Saint-Étienne – Stade Geoffroy-Guichard
FRANCE v URUGUAY	Thu, 14 Sept – 21:00	Lille – Stade Pierre-Mauroy
NEW ZEALAND v NAMIBIA	Fri, 15 Sept – 21:00	Toulouse – Stadium de Toulouse
ITALY v URUGUAY	Wed, 20 Sept – 17:45	Nice – Stade de Nice
FRANCE v NAMIBIA	Thu, 21 Sept – 21:00	Marseille – Stade Vélodrome
URUGUAY v NAMIBIA	Wed, 27 Sept – 17:45	Lyon – OL Stadium
NEW ZEALAND v ITALY	Fri, 29 Sept – 21:00	Lyon – OL Stadium
NEW ZEALAND v URUGUAY	Thu, 5 Oct – 21:00	Lyon – OL Stadium
FRANCE v ITALY	Fri, 6 Oct – 21:00	Lyon – OL Stadium

POOL B

SOUTH AFRICA
IRELAND
SCOTLAND
TONGA
ROMANIA

IRELAND v ROMANIA	Sat, 9 Sept – 15:30	Bordeaux – Stade de Bordeaux
SOUTH AFRICA v SCOTLAND	Sun, 10 Sept – 17:45	Marseille – Stade Vélodrome
IRELAND v TONGA	Sat, 16 Sept – 21:00	Nantes – Stade de la Beaujoire
SOUTH AFRICA v ROMANIA	Sun, 17 Sept – 15:00	Bordeaux – Stade de Bordeaux
SOUTH AFRICA v IRELAND	Sat, 23 Sept – 21:00	Saint-Denis – Stade de France
SCOTLAND v TONGA	Sun, 24 Sept – 17:45	Nice – Stade de Nice
SCOTLAND v ROMANIA	Sat, 30 Sept – 21:00	Lille – Stade Pierre-Mauroy
SOUTH AFRICA v TONGA	Sun, 1 Oct – 21:00	Marseille – Stade Vélodrome
IRELAND v SCOTLAND	Sat, 7 Oct – 21:00	Saint-Denis – Stade de France
TONGA v ROMANIA	Sun, 8 Oct – 17:45	Lille – Stade Pierre-Mauroy

QUARTER-FINAL 1

Sat, 14 Oct – 17:00
Marseille – Stade Vélodrome

WINNER POOL C
v
RUNNER-UP POOL D

QUARTER-FINAL 2

Sat, 14 Oct – 21:00
Saint-Denis – Stade de France

WINNER POOL B
v
RUNNER-UP POOL A

QUARTER-FINAL 3

Sun, 15 Oct – 17:00
Marseille – Stade Vélodrome

WINNER POOL D
v
RUNNER-UP POOL C

QUARTER-FINAL 4

Sun, 15 Oct – 21:00
Saint-Denis – Stade de France

WINNER POOL A
v
RUNNER-UP POOL B

ALL MATCHES ARE CET (UTC +1). SUBJECT TO CHANGE.

TOURNAMENT WALL CHART

POOL C

WALES
AUSTRALIA
FIJI
GEORGIA
PORTUGAL

AUSTRALIA v GEORGIA
Sat, 9 Sept - 18:00
Saint-Denis - Stade de France

WALES v FIJI
Sun, 10 Sept - 21:00
Bordeaux - Stade de Bordeaux

WALES v PORTUGAL
Sat, 16 Sept - 17:45
Nice - Stade de Nice

AUSTRALIA v FIJI
Sun, 17 Sept - 17:45
Saint-Étienne - Stade Geoffroy-Guichard

GEORGIA v PORTUGAL
Sat, 23 Sept - 14:00
Toulouse - Stadium de Toulouse

WALES v AUSTRALIA
Sun, 24 Sept - 21:00
Lyon - OL Stadium

FIJI v GEORGIA
Sat, 30 Sept - 17:45
Bordeaux - Stade de Bordeaux

AUSTRALIA v PORTUGAL
Sun, 1 Oct - 17:45
Saint-Étienne - Stade Geoffroy-Guichard

WALES v GEORGIA
Sat, 7 Oct - 15:00
Nantes - Stade de la Beaujoire

FIJI v PORTUGAL
Sun, 8 Oct - 21:00
Toulouse - Stadium de Toulouse

POOL D

ENGLAND
JAPAN
ARGENTINA
SAMOA
CHILE

ENGLAND v ARGENTINA
Sat, 9 Sept - 21:00
Marseille - Stade Vélodrome

JAPAN v CHILE
Sun, 10 Sept - 13:00
Toulouse - Stadium de Toulouse

SAMOA v CHILE
Sat, 16 Sept - 15:00
Bordeaux - Stade de Bordeaux

ENGLAND v JAPAN
Sun, 17 Sept - 21:00
Nice - Stade de Nice

ARGENTINA v SAMOA
Fri, 22 Sept - 17:45
Saint-Étienne - Stade Geoffroy-Guichard

ENGLAND v CHILE
Sat, 23 Sept - 17:45
Lille - Stade Pierre-Mauroy

JAPAN v SAMOA
Thu, 28 Sept - 21:00
Toulouse - Stadium de Toulouse

ARGENTINA v CHILE
Sat, 30 Sept - 15:00
Nantes - Stade de la Beaujoire

ENGLAND v SAMOA
Sat, 7 Oct - 17:45
Lille - Stade Pierre-Mauroy

JAPAN v ARGENTINA
Sun, 8 Oct - 13:00
Nantes - Stade de la Beaujoire

SEMI-FINAL 1

Fri, 20 Oct - 21:00
Saint-Denis - Stade de France

WINNER QF 1 
v
WINNER QF 2

SEMI-FINAL 2

Sat, 21 Oct - 21:00
Saint-Denis - Stade de France

WINNER QF 3
v
WINNER QF 4

BRONZE FINAL

Fri, 27 Oct - 21:00
Saint-Denis - Stade de France

LOSER SF 1
v
LOSER SF 2

FINAL

Sat, 28 Oct - 21:00
Saint-Denis - Stade de France

WINNER SF 1
v
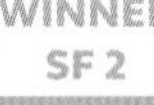
WINNER SF 2

Credits

The publishers would like to thank the following sources for their kind permission to reproduce the pictures in this book. (T-top, B-bottom, L-left, R-right, C-centre)

ALL © GETTY IMAGES: AFP 100; Odd Andersen/AFP 109, 122; Steve Bardens/World Rugby 50L, 59, 73; Lou Benoist/AFP 19TR; Shaun Botterill 76L; Gabriel Bouys/AFP 40BR; Mike Brett/Popperfoto 44-45; Simon Bruty 102, 105, 120-121; Lynne Cameron 43; Ramsey Cardy/Sportsfile 11, 34BR, 62BR; Steve Christo/Corbis 60BR; Russell Cheyne 60L, 103; Emmanuele Ciancaglini/CPS Images 88; Tim Clayton/Corbis 80-81; Alex Davidson/RFU 70BR, 94; Anthony Dibon/Icon Sport 17BR; Alexandre Dimou/Icon Sport 21BR; Martin Dokoupil/World Rugby 29, 67; Fred Dufour/AFP 66L; Baptiste Fernandez/Icon Sport 17TR, 21TR, 64BR, 66BR; Franck Fife/AFP 111; Stu Forster 42BR, 47, 48L, 63, 71, 82-83, 89; Georges Gobet/AFP 14, 101; Laurence Griffiths 115; Pascal Guyot/AFP 52L; Richard Heathcote 10; Richard Heathcote/World Rugby 54L, 58BR, 114, 123, 124; Marcelo Hernandez 24-25; Mike Hewitt/World Rugby 36L; Ryan Hiscott 74BR; Richard Huggard/Gallo Images 46BR; Tom Jenkins 125; Matt Lewis/World Rugby 54BR, 64L; Christian Liewig/Corbis 8-9, 68-69; Warren Little 62L; Warren Little/World Rugby 30, 40L, 96-97; Alex Livesey/Federugby 38BR; Marcio Machado/Eurasia Sport Images 18TR; Craig Mercer/MB Media 75; Mark Metcalfe/World Rugby 34L; Aurelien Meunier/World Rugby 4, 12; Vasile Mihai-Antonio/World Rugby 28; Tyler Miller/Sportsfile 78BR; Brendan Moran/Sportsfile 48BR, 49, 87; Pablo Morano/MB Media 32-33, 36BR; Olivier Morin/AFP 107; Dan Mullan 61; Francois Nel/World Rugby 31, 50BR; Peter Parkes/AFP 70L; Hannah Peters 26, 90; Hugo Pfeiffer/Icon Sport 18BR, 19BR; Tertius Pickard/Gallo Images 110; Ryan Pierse 58L; Adam Pretty 53, 98-99; David Ramos/World Rugby 35, 42L, 118-119; Chris Roberts 20B; David Rogers 6, 85, 86, 95, 113; David Rogers/World Rugby 104, 108, 112; Timothy Rogers 39; Clive Rose/World Rugby 7, 46L, 51, 72L, 72BR, 91, 92, 116, 117; Dave Rowland 52BR, 77; Christophe Simon/AFP 38L; Cameron Spencer 15, 41, 74L, 93; Michael Steele 55; Bob Thomas Sports Photography 22-23, 56-57; Javier Torres/AFP 78L, 79; Levan Verdzeuli 65; Peter Wallis/World Rugby 27; Phil Walter 76BR; Nick Wilson/World Rugby 106; Dave Winter/Icon Sport 20TR, 37, 84; World Rugby 13

Cover photographs: ALL © GETTY IMAGES
Front cover: (Ardie Savea & Maro Itoje) David Rogers; (Siya Kolisi) Adam Pretty; (Jonathan Sexton) Brendan Moran/Sportsfile; (Michael Cooper) Mark Kolbe.
Back cover: (Japan v Sscotland action, RWC 2019) Kaz Photography; (France v Tonga action, RWC 2019) Franck Fife/AFP; (Fiji v Wales action, RWC 2019) Koki Nagahama.

Every effort has been made to acknowledge correctly and contact the source and/or copyright holder of each picture. Any unintentional errors or omissions will be corrected in future editions of this book.